Soup

By Coralie Castle
Illustrated by Roy Killeen
Pitman Publishing

Published in the United States by 101 Productions
First published in Great Britain 1976

Pitman Publishing Limited
Pitman House, 39 Parker Street, London WC2B 5PB

Sir Isaac Pitman and Sons Limited
Banda Street, P.O. Box 46038, Nairobi, Kenya

Pitman Publishing Co. S.A. (Pty) Limited
Craighall Mews, Jan Smuts Avenue, Craighall Park,
Johannesburg 2001, South Africa

British edition prepared by Helena Radecka

ISBN: 0 273 00963 X

G116:17

Text set in 11/13 pt. IBM Press Roman, printed by
photolithography, and bound in Great Britain at
The Pitman Press, Bath

Contents

Spirit of Soups Past

"One wit, like a knuckle of ham in the soup, gives zest to the dish, but more than one serves only to spoil the pottage."
                                —Tobias Smollett

Soup is at least as old as the art of cookery, and probably older, in the form of cold concoctions of gruel or pottage. Early references to it are, however, few and far between. One legend supposes that beer was invented accidentally when an ancient Egyptian cook let a bowl of gruel stand too long in the sun. and ever since there has been much more written about alcoholic beverages than lowly soup.

Esau, in selling his birthright to Jacob for the pottage of red lentils, was considered a fool. Elisha performed a miracle when he cast meal into a pottage of poisonous boiled wild gourds "and then there was no harm in it." The Israelites made a purée of manna, which some scholars believe to have been secretion from the tamarisk plant, but there is little other biblical reference to soup except when Isaiah wrote, "and broth of abominable things is in their vessels." References to soups show up all over the world. As far back as 2000 B.C., Vedic literature in India mentioned parched barley ground up with juices. Mayan Indians used maize for various liquid foods, most at least mildly alcoholic. Early North American Indians made a broth of hickory-nut milk. Yosemite Indians shredded fungi for mushroom soup and also cooked horse-chestnut gruel. Eskimos still relish fatty soup laced with seal or caribou blood.

ANCIENT GREECE AND ROME

The Greeks and Romans produced a few historians interested in all kinds of food, including soup. Over 2,500 years ago, in Greece, soups of beans, peas, or lentils relieved the monotony of "bread and a relish," and hot pea soup could be bought in the streets. Kykeon (barley meal, grated cheese and wine) served as a ritual beverage at the mysteries of Eleusis. Black Broth, made of pork, blood, vinegar, salt and heavy seasoning was a main dish.

The earliest cookery book in existence is attributed to Apicius, a first-century Roman. His barley soup was made by boiling crushed barley with lentils, peas and chick peas. He mentions a purée of lettuce leaves and onions. There was also a liquid sweet-fruit dish of apricots cooked in honey, passum (dried grapes and must), wine and vinegar flavored with pepper, mint and a little liquamen (strained liquid from salted-down fish entrails, available commercially in pots as early as 400 B.C.). Apicius is said to have killed himself when his fortune ran out and he could no longer afford expensive foods. It was Athenaeus in about A.D. 200 who wrote extensively about food, seasonings and soup. His "Deipnosophistae" (deipno - dining; sophistis - sage) recounts endless dinner conversations which range over many subjects. Here are a few samples:

" 'No Lentils bring to me. They do taint the breath `—no expensive dishes, but any of those vulgar lentils or what is called lentil soup.' And when everyone laughed, especially at the idea of lentil soup, he said, 'You are very ignorant men, you feasters, never having read any books of the Silli or Timon the Pyrrhonian. For he speaks of lentil soup as follows':

The Teian barley-cakes do please me not,
Nor e'en the Lydian sauces: but the Greeks,
And their dry lentil soup, delight me more
Than all that painful luxury of excess."

THE MIDDLE AGES TO MODERN SOUPS

In early times soup was called pottage (from pot and the latin *potare,* to drink). But during the Middle Ages the word "soup" established itself in almost every European language, largely supplanting "pottage" except for "potage" in France. Some

5

variations are: *Soop, sopa, sope, soepe, suppa, soppe, soep, suppe, soppa, sopero, soupe, chupe, zuppa, zup.* To "sup" was to eat the evening meal at which soup was traditionally served, and the meal itself became "supper."

In 1475, a Venetian by the name of Platina published "De Honesta Voluptate," a cookbook and guide to living with "honest indulgence and good health." With some ingenuousness, he commented on the merits of various foods. For example, according to him, lentils generate black bile and cause leprosy, while turnips "soothe the throat and arouse the passion."

His soup recipes range from potages of livers, lungs and intestines to Verzusum, a sweet soup that "cools the liver and checks the bile." White broth contained a pound of ground almonds, 10 egg whites and two loaves of softened white bread. Soups were always to be kept far enough away from the coals so as not to absorb the smoke. Many of them called for verjuice (acid liquor from sour fruit juice) or must (unfermented wine). Even though he said hemp potage was difficult to digest and caused squeamishness, its elaborate recipe was included, as well as one for an eel torta, which was to be served to one's enemies because it was so bad.

In 1669, "The Closet" of the Eminent Learned Sir Kenelme Digbie Kt., was published in London, and contained the following soup recipes: *"Barley Pôtage* — Take half a pound of French-barley, and wash it in three or four hot waters; then tye it up in a course linnen-cloth and strike it five or six blows against the table; for this will make it very tender . . . and let it mittoner a while upon the Chafing-dish, then serve it in."

"Portugal Broth, as it was made for the Queen — Make a very good broth with some lean of Veal, Beef and Mutton, and with a brawny Hen or young Cock. . . . . and when the broth is very good, you may drink it so, or, pour a little of it upon tosted sliced bread, and stew it, till the bread have drunk up all that broth, then add a little more, and stew; so adding by little and little, that the bread may imbibe it and swell: whereas if you drown it at once, the bread will not swell, and grow like gelly."

"Potage de santé of Mounsieur de S. Eurement. Put a knuckle of Veal and a Hen into an earthen Pipkin with a Gallon of water (about nine of the Clock forenoon) and boil it gently. When no more scum riseth (which will be in about a quarter of an hour,) take out the Hen (which else would be too much boiled,) and continue boiling gently till about half an hour past ten. Then put in the Hen again, and a handful of white Endive. Near half hour after eleven, put in two good handfuls of tender Sorrel, Borage, Bugloss, Lettice, Purslane a handful a piece, a little Cerfevil, and a little Beet-leaves. When he is in pretty good health, that he may venture upon more savoury hotter things, he puts in a large Onion stuck round with Cloves, and sometimes a little bundle of Thyme and other hot savoury herbs; which let boil a good half hour or better, and take them out, and throw them away. . . . . .

"The Queen Mothers *Pressis Nourissant* was thus made. Take un Gigot of Mutton, a piece of Veal, and a Capon (or half the quantity of each of these) and put them on rost with convenient fire, till they are above half rosted, or rather, till they be two thirds rosted. Then take them off, and squeese out all their juyce in a press with screws, and scum all the fat from it, and put it between two dishes upon a Chafing-dish of Coals to boil a very little, or rather but to heat well; for by then it is through hot, the juyce will be ripened enough to drink, where-as

6

before it was raw and bloody; then if you perceive any fat to remain and swim upon it, cleanse it away with a Feather. Sqeese the juyce of an Orange (through a holed spoon) into half a Porrenger full of this, and add a little Salt, and drink it. The Queen used this at nights in stead of a Supper; for when she took this, she did eat nothing else. It is of great, yet temperate nourishment. If you take a couple of Partridges in stead of a Capon, it will be of more nourishment, but hotter. Great Weaknesses and Consumptions have been recovered with long use of this, and strength and long life continued notably. It is good to take two or three spoonfuls of it in a good ordinary bouillon. I should like better the boiling the same things in a close flagon in bulliente Balneos as my Lady Kent, and My Mother used."

During the 18th century, references to soup occasionally appeared in English literature. In Jonathan Swift's "Directions to Servants" (1745) he advised the cook: "If your Dinner miscarrieth in almost every Dish, how could you help it? You were seized by the Footmen coming into the Kitchen; and, to prove it true, take Occasion to be angry, and throw a Ladle-full of Broth on one or two of their Liveries . . ." The British Navy's famous "portable soup" was also developed in the 18th century. The variety carried by Captain Cook on his circumnavigation of 1772–75 was described by the President of the Royal Society, Sir John Pringle, as being " . . . reduced to the consistency of a glue, which in effect it is."

By the 19th century, the word "soup" had become the source of some strange expressions. The term "soup-shop," according to the London Journal, referred to those establishments where burglars and thieves disposed of any silver or gold plate which fell into their hands. In such places, the melting pots were always kept ready. In Ireland, Protestant clergymen who sought converts by dispensing soup as charity were called "soupers." In 1890, the Catholic News commented, "Our readers are no doubt aware of the usual falsehoods employed by soupers for this purpose."

Meanwhile, 1890 Chicagoans were presumably poring over a newly published "Compendium of Cookery together with the Book of Knowledge, or 1000 ways of getting rich." Along with the Bible it apparently handled all of life's problems. It offers a "tonic for reformed drunkards to restore the vigor of the stomach." On the other hand it prescribes: "Fever and Ague — Four ounces galangal-root in a quart of gin, steeped in a warm place; take often."

More intriguing is its advice on how "To Restore From Stroke of Lightning — Shower with cold water for two hours; if the patient does not show signs of life, put salt in the water, and continue to shower an hour longer." What then? Its soups section sounds a little more practical:

• *Stock Soup* — .... basis of many of the soups . . . . . Time: Five and one-half hours. Average cost, twenty-five cents per quart.

• *White Stock Soup* — .... Strain off the liquor; rub the vegetables through the colander . . . . . and, as is your Saturday custom, put into a wide-mouth jar or a large bowl. . . .

Potatoes, if boiled in the soup, are thought by some to render it unwholesome, from the opinion that the water in which potatoes have been cooked is almost a poison.

• *Mutton Soup* — Three pounds perfectly lean mutton. The scrag makes good soup and costs little. Two or three pounds of bones well pounded . . . . . Send around grated cheese with this soup.

- *Chicken Cream Soup* — Boil an old fowl, with an onion, in four quarts of cold water, until there remain but two quarts . . . .
- *Potato Soup* — Get as many beef or ham bones as you can, and smash them into fragments . . . .
- *Game Soup* — Two grouse or partridges, or if you have neither, use a pair of rabbits . . . . .

Simultaneously in San Francisco was published: "Scammell's Universal Treasure-House of Useful Knowledge, an Encyclopedia of Valuable Receipts in the Principal Arts of Life, including complete treatises on Practical chemistry; the prevention and cure of disease; household and culinary art; agriculture and stock-raising; the mechanical arts; mercantile life and laws; arts of refinement; recreations, etc." The soups include:

- *Calf's Head* — Parboil a calf's head; take off the skin and cut it into pieces of about 1-1/2" square; mince the fleshy part into smaller pieces; take out the back part of the eyes, and cut the remainder into rings; skin the tongue; cut it into slices; turn the whole into 3 qts of good stock . . . . .
- *Celery* — 9 heads of celery; 1 teaspoonful of salt, nutmeg to taste,; 1 lump of sugar; 1/2 pt. of strong stock; 1 pt. of cream; 2 qts. of boiling water; cut the celery into small pieces; throw it into the water . . . .
- *Lentil* — Take 3/4 lb. of lentils; pick, wash and set on the fire with cold water, just enough to cover; do not cook in an earthen pot, as they will not get soft . . . .
- *Consommé* — 6 lbs of lean beef; an old fowl, with the giblets, and any pieces of bone that you may have . . . . .
- *Curry* — Cut the meat from an ox cheek; soak it well . . . .
- *French* — Clean nicely a sheep's head . . . . . strain all off; cut the head into pieces and serve in the soup.
- *Herb* — Slice 3 large but young cucumbers; a handful of spring onions and six lettuces . . . . .
- *Mock Turtle* — Take 1/2 a calf's head . . . . procure a tin of mock turtle soup, boil this up with stock . . . The mixture of the stock made from fresh vegetables, with the preserved soup, will correct the slight taste of tin, which is the only objection which can be urged against it; and when a small quantity only of soup is required it will save time, trouble and expense to make it in this way, rather than to prepare it at home.
- *Mutton* — Take a shoulder of good heavy mutton weighing about 4 lbs; remove the skin and fat . . . . .
- *Pepper Pot* — Put 4 cow's feet and 4 lbs. of tripe to boil with water to cover them . . . . .

For years cookbook writers apparently felt responsibility for far more than food, and readers valued such books highly.

"The White House Cook Book, a comprehensive cyclopedia of information for the home containing cooking, toilet and household recipes, menus, dinner-giving, table etiquette, care of the sick, health suggestions, facts worth knowing, etc." was published in the USA in 1905 and dedicated 'To the wives of Our Presidents, those noble women who have graced the White House.' " One copy was inscribed by its owner, "This book belongs to Mrs. Nellie P. Doane, she wants it and needs it and is a scratching, biting, kicking hairpuller. So beware."

Among the soup recipes are the following:

- *Plain Economical Soup* — Take a cold roastbeef bone etc., ... Serve this soup with sippits of toast. Sippits are bits of dry toast cut into a triangular form. A seasonable dish about the holidays.

• *Corn Soup* — Cut the corn from the cob, and boil the cobs in water for at least an hour, then add the grains .....

• *Squirrel Soup* — Wash and quarter three or four good sized squirrels; put them on, with a small tablespoonful of salt, directly after breakfast in a gallon of cold water. Cover the pot close .....

• *Mock Turtle Soup, of Calf's Head* — Scald a well-cleansed Calf's head, remove the brain, tie it up in a cloth, and boil an hour, or until the meat will easily slip from the bone .....

• *Green Turtle Soup* — After removing the entrails, cut up the coarser parts of the turtle meat and bones. Add four quarts of water ..... At the end of four hours strain the soup, and add the inner parts of the turtle and the green fat ..... If there are eggs in the turtle, boil them in a separate vessel for four hours, and throw into the soup before taking up .... Some cooks put in the green fat, cut into lumps

an inch long. This makes a handsomer soup. Green turtle can now be purchased preserved in air-tight cans.

The Corona Club Cookbook, published in San Francisco in 1910 contains the following:

• *Wine Soup* — One quart boiling water, 1/2 teacupful of sago, the peeling of 1/2 a lemon; boil until sago is done, then add 1 teacupful of claret wine and sugar to taste.

• *Scraped Beef in Broth* — Buy 1/4 of a pound of round steak; be careful none of the dried edges of the meat are included in your purchase, as this sometimes poisons babies. Sear on hot griddle to retain the juice. Split in two and scrape with a dull knife so that only the pulp and none of the fibre is retained. Put in broth with rice.

According to Escoffier, soups were considered commonplace until this century. Today, however, soup is not only firmly established as part of a fashionable meal, but also is popular as a meal in itself. Our ancestors would be amazed and delighted, I think, if they were to taste all of the varied soups that follow.

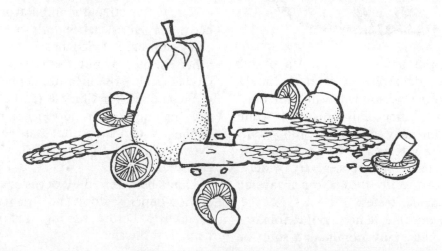

Between the Lines

One person, tasting a soup with the tip of his tongue and inhaling its aroma, may immediately smile or frown. Another person will wait until all of his tastebuds report, then will ponder a while before judging. Both may reverse their opinions after noting lingering aftertastes. Not only tasting methods, but also taste preferences vary widely. luckily, soups, unlike angelfood cake, can always be adjusted to suit particular tastes.

Certain distinct flavors like lemon, garlic, tomato, pepper and cumin can easily dominate a soup or offend ordinary palates if used to excess. Therefore, soup demands a light touch. After all, a sorrel soup should taste like sorrel, an avocado like avocado, and no one wants a guest to say, "Ugh!" A light touch with servings is equally important. An overpowering portion can turn even the finest soup into a disaster. For a Maharajah offer more curry; for a Latin-American, more chili powder; for a gourmand, another serving.

Don't let prejudices hem you in. Distasteful seasonings can blend delightfully into unfamiliar surroundings. A new try at a food given up at age ten may be a pleasant surprise. Use each recipe as it is before improvising.

• Some flavors blend; some complement and retain their identity; some merely clash or cancel each other. Certain seasonings don't come out without long steeping; others fade fast and must be added at the last minute.

• Cold soups flooding the tongue with soothing coolness slowly contact tastebuds which hot soups rarely reach, permitting appreciation of more delicate flavors. Hot soups tend to travel quickly along the top of the tongue for immediate swallowing and need stronger seasoning.

• Know the strength and flavor of each of your herbs and spices, particularly blended powders like curry and chili. Dried herbs should be used unless otherwise noted, but fresh are a delight and easily grown. Treble the measurements when using fresh.

• Fresh chives or Chinese (garlic) chives are worth growing outdoors or indoors in a pot.

• Many's the soup that has been changed from "very good" to "spectacular" with tasty, colorful garnishes.

• Don't be deterred by occasional unpleasant preparation odors; seafood and Oriental soups will purge themselves before serving. Let your exhaust fan help clear the air.

• Use freshly grated nutmeg, black pepper and cheese. If you prefer coarsely ground salt, grind up sea salt crystals (available in health food shops). Peppercorns release more flavor if crushed before using when recipes call for whole peppercorns.

• A bitter cucumber will ruin a soup. Taste first.

• If your blender won't purée smoothly, sieve afterwards when you want smooth texture.

• Tailor portions and select containers to fit the occasion—brunch, main lunch dish, dinner overture, midnight snack, etc.— and the weather.

• Vegetarians will find substituting vegetable stock and perhaps fortifying with vegetable stock cubes in any recipe gives a flavorful soup.

Whether using whole, crushed or chopped, smash garlic cloves with the flat of a large knife or cleaver to remove skin easily and release more juices.

• Shallots are special and impart a unique flavor, so better not use a substitute.

• When thickening a soup with egg yolks and cream, always wait until the last minute; reheating or keeping warm will curdle the soup.

• Sorrel is not yet available in most markets, but is easily grown and does grow wild if you know where to find it. Although I have never used bottled or canned sorrel I understand it can be substituted.

• Try growing your own watercress or curlycress in a shady spot with lots of water. It reseeds itself and you always have a last-minute garnish.

• Chervil, if seeds are fresh and sun is not too hot, grows as well as parsley. It's more feathery with a delicate liquorice flavor that is quite different.

• Flat leaf parsley is not as pretty as the curly variety for garnishing, but it has a stronger flavor and is just as easy to grow. Be sure to cut some stems when using parsley in cooking, as the flavor is stronger in the stems.

• See how gelatinous your stock is before making a cold soup. If it may make the soup too thick, thin with water and stock base before using.

• Bouquet garni: Tie the herbs up in cheesecloth for easy removal from pot.

• Chinese parsley, cilantro and fresh coriander are the same. The taste is unique and not favored by all. The flavor varies with the age of the plant and as you become used to it you might change your mind if at first you didn't like it. Easily grown at home.

Treat as chervil and use the stems as with parsley.

• All pasta products should be cooked *al dente!*

• Use the modern, light touch in cooking vegetables that are to retain their identity. Serve them tender-crisp, not mushy.

• Blanching is parboiling one to three minutes, then draining. When used to partially cook vegetables, a cold-water rinse stops cooking at the desired point. When blanching scum-prone ingredients like veal bones, rinse well after draining, then add to fresh cooking water in a clean pot.

• Good chicken stock cubes are hard to find, but they are extremely useful for thinning down gelatinous stocks without diluted flavor, or for adding extra flavor when needed.

Stocks and Clear Soups

Some foods are for lovers, some for philosophers,
some for tax collectors . . .
When one is near the grave, I prepare for him
some lentil soup, and make the crowning
meal of his life glorious.

—Athenaeus, circa 200 B.C.

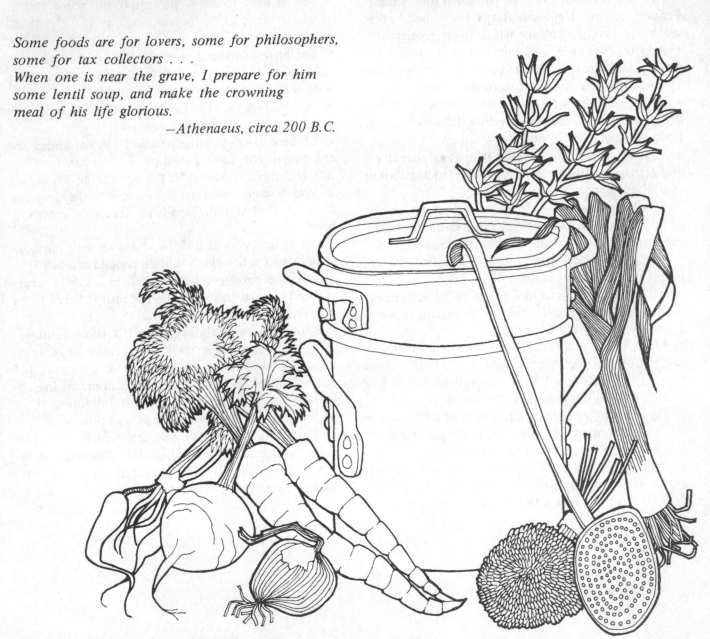

STOCKS AND CLEAR SOUPS

Simmer selected raw, precooked, or leftover morsels in water with butter or wine. Skim, strain out the leached solids, and season if desired. Cool, then refrigerate. Remove the solidified fat and you have the liquor or broth so vital to every soup chef—stock.

Sounds simple—until you consider the complexity of possible ingredients and flavors. While proportions are inexact, merely tossing anything and everything into a pot is not the answer. The ingredients must be good ones and they must be treated with care.

BASIC STOCKS

Leftovers: Bones, scraps, carcasses, unserved portions, gravies, vegetable cooking water, vegetable tops, leaves and peelings all are valuable in making stock as long as they're clean and kept refrigerated until added to the pot. Recycling in the kitchen is more than just an economy, it's a system of flavor saving, of cooking with your own array of delicious concentrates that are continually being modified, added to, and blended. Stocks are the flavor key not only to soups, but to many other gourmet dishes as well. For example, boiling fresh or frozen vegetables in stock instead of plain water.

Cooking: Cut up bones if possible. Start with cold water, cover, bring slowly to a rapid boil. Skim off any scum that rises to the surface. Turn down the heat and simmer, covered, 2 hours for leftover bones, 4 hours for fresh, adding vegetables and seasoning at the halfway point. Strain through coarse sieve into another saucepan, then through a finer one into jars. Cool completely, put lids on jars, label, and refrigerate.

Storing: Fat acts as a sealer and solidifies under refrigeration, making it easy to remove. If stock is not used within ten days, it's best to return to the pot for a 2-minute boil, after which it can be refrigerated again. Stock can be frozen, but because freezing causes ingredients to separate it should be brought to a boil before using.

Defatting: If fresh stock is to be used immediately, skim off as much surface fat as possible, then float an ice cube to congeal the rest. A piece of chilled lettuce will collect fat on its surface.

Clarifying: To each 1-1/2 pints stock add 1 egg white beaten slightly with 2 teaspoons cold water and 1 crumbled egg shell. Stir and heat to boiling. Boil 2 minutes, remove from heat and let stand without stirring 20 minutes. Pour through strainer lined with double cheesecloth.

Concentrating: For richer, more flavorful stock, boil down strained stock to reduce water content.

Stocks from Fresh Bones

VEAL STOCK

2 pounds veal knuckle bone with meat, cut up
2 pounds veal shin bones, cut up
1 pair pig's trotters (optional)
6 pints water
2 carrots, chopped
2 onions, chopped
2 leeks and some tops, chopped
2 celery stalks and tops, chopped
2 turnips, chopped (optional)
2 garlic cloves (optional)
6 parsley sprigs
1 thyme sprig
1 bay leaf
2 teaspoons salt
6 peppercorns
1/2 teaspoon turmeric

White Stock:
Cover bones with 3 pints of the water, bring to rapid boil, drain and rinse bones. Return to clean soup pan and add 3 pints fresh water. Cover, bring slowly to rapid boil, skim off any more scum that may rise to top, cover, and simmer 2 hours.
Add remaining ingredients and simmer 2 hours. Strain, jar, cool, cover and refrigerate. Makes about 2-1/2 pints.

Brown Veal Stock:
Brown bones in 3 tablespoons oil and/or butter. Simmer 2 hours, add browned vegetables and continue cooking 2 more hours.

BEEF STOCK

4 pounds beef bones with meat, cut up
1 - 2 pounds marrow bones, sawed into 3-inch pieces
1 pair pig's trotters (optional)
5 pints cold water

3 carrots, chopped
2 celery stalks and tops, chopped
2 turnips, chopped
2 whole onions, each stuck with 2 cloves
6–8 tablespoons diced tomatoes (optional)
4 tablespoons diced green pepper (optional)
6 parsley sprigs
1 thyme sprig
1 oregano or marjoram sprig
1 bay leaf
2 cloves garlic (optional)
6 peppercorns
1 tablespoon salt

Brown Stock:
Put bones and pig's trotters in a large pan and add water. Cover pan, bring slowly to rapid boil, skim off any scum and simmer 2 hours.
Add rest of ingredients and continue cooking 2 more hours. Strain, jar, cool, cover and refrigerate. Makes about 4 pints.

Dark Beef Stock:
Brown bones in butter and/or oil in the pan or a hot oven. Add browned vegetables after 2 hours.

CHICKEN STOCK

6 pounds chicken backs, necks, and wing tips,
  or 1 large boiling fowl, cut up
5 pints cold water
2 onions, chopped
2 carrots, chopped
1 turnip, chopped
2 celery stalks and tops, chopped
2 leeks and tops, chopped
2 garlic cloves
1 bay leaf
6 parsley sprigs
1 thyme sprig
1 savory sprig
1 tablespoon salt
1 teaspoon turmeric
1/2 teaspoon poultry seasoning

White Stock:
Put bones and water in a saucepan, cover and bring slowly to rapid boil. Skim off any scum that may rise to top and simmer 2 hours.
Add remaining ingredients and simmer 2 more hours. Strain, jar, cool, cover and refrigerate. Makes a generous 3 pints.

Brown Chicken Stock:
Brown bones in 3 tablespoons butter and/or rendered chicken fat in the pan or a hot oven. Simmer 2 hours, add browned vegetables, and continue cooking 2 more hours.

PORK STOCK

Follow directions for chicken stock, substituting pork bones for chicken bones, sage for turmeric; add 1 oregano or marjoram sprig.

LAMB STOCK

Follow directions for beef stock, substituting meaty lamb bones for the beef and adding 1 sprig rosemary.

VEGETABLE STOCK

Use twice as much liquid as vegetables. Brown vegetables or not, as preferred, and use leftovers if desired. Tomatoes, lettuce, parsnips, leeks, turnips, broccoli stems, green pea pods, green beans, carrots, onions, asparagus ends, spring onion tops, herbs and spices.

FISH STOCK

3/4 pint each white wine and water
2 pounds fish heads, bones, shells
1 onion, chopped
3 parsley sprigs
1 bay leaf
1 thyme sprig
2 tablespoons lemon juice
1/2 teaspoon tarragon
1 teaspoon grated lemon peel
6 peppercorns
2 cloves
6—8 tablespoons chopped mushroom stems
1 teaspoon salt
1 tablespoon butter or oil

Combine ingredients in a pan, cover, bring to boil, skim off surface scum and simmer 1 hour.
Strain, jar, cook, cover and refrigerate. Makes about 1 pint.

STOCK FROM ROAST BEEF

6 or 7 cracked ribs of leftover rib roast of beef and
  any scraps
2 onions, chopped
2 carrots, chopped
2 stalks celery and tops, chopped
2 leeks, chopped
2 garlic cloves (optional)
3 tablespoons oil and/or rendered beef fat
6 peppercorns
8 parsley sprigs
1 thyme sprig
1 marjoram sprig
1 bay leaf
1/2 tablespoon salt
6—8 tablespoons chopped mushroom stems
generous 3 pints cold water

Brown onions, carrots, celery and leeks in oil and/
or fat. Add to the pan with rest of ingredients,
cover, bring slowly to rapid boil, skim off any scum
that rises to the top, cover and simmer 2 hours.
Strain, jar, cook, cover and refrigerate. Makes about
2 pints.

LAMB STOCK

Follow directions for roast beef stock, using leftover leg of lamb bones and scraps instead of beef
bones; add 1 sprig rosemary and 1 sprig oregano.

PORK STOCK

Follow directions for roast beef stock, using leftover pork bones and adding 1 teaspoon sage and 1
sprig oregano or marjoram.

POULTRY STOCK

1 turkey carcass, or 2 chicken or duck carcasses
  plus any leftover scraps and giblets
2 onions, chopped
2 carrots, chopped
2 leeks, chopped
2 turnips, chopped
1 garlic clove
6 parsley sprigs
1 thyme sprig
1 bay leaf
6 peppercorns
1/2 tablespoon salt
1/2 teaspoon each poultry seasoning and turmeric
5 pints cold water

Put all ingredients in a saucepan, cover and bring
slowly to rapid boil. Skim off any scum that may
rise to top, cover and simmer 2 hours. Strain, jar,
cool, cover and refrigerate. Makes a generous 3 pints.

GAME STOCK

4 pounds venison bones and scraps, or pheasant
  or partridge carcasses, or rabbit bones,
  plus scraps and giblets
  (add veal knuckle bone if needed to
  make 4 pounds)
2 onions, chopped
2 carrots, chopped
2 celery stalks, chopped
1/4 pound salt pork, diced and blanched
2 garlic cloves
1 teaspoon salt
6 parsley sprigs
1 thyme sprig
1 bay leaf
2 cloves
1 teaspoon basil
4 peppercorns
1/2 teaspoon juniper berries (optional)
5 pints cold water

Put all ingredients in a large pan. Cover, bring
slowly to rapid boil, skim off any scum that may
rise to top, cover and simmer 2 hours. Strain and
boil to reduce to 3 pints or less, as desired.
Jar, cool and refrigerate. Remove fat and clarify
before using.

BOUILLON

Follow recipe for dark beef stock, adding 1 pound cut-up beef and 1 meaty veal knuckle. Simmer 5 hours, strain, chill, defat and clarify. Add dry sherry and Worcestershire sauce to taste.
Serves 6

BEEF CONSOMMÉ

Follow recipe for dark beef stock, adding 1 large meaty veal knuckle and 1 pound chicken giblets. Strain, reduce to concentrate, chill, defat and clarify.
Serves 6

PETITE MARMITE

Follow general rule for making stock, using 1-1/2 pounds shin of beef, cubed, 1 meaty veal knuckle, cut up, 2 beef bones, cut up, 1 pound chicken giblets, 4 pints water, 1 tablespoon salt, 3 peppercorns, 4 parsley sprigs and 1 thyme sprig. Cook 1 hour, add 2 chopped carrots, 1 chopped turnip, 1 chopped leek and some green, 1 onion stuck with 2 cloves, and 2 stalks chopped celery and leaves. Cook 2 hours, strain, chill, defat and clarify.
Serves 6

JELLIED BOUILLON

Soften 2 tablespoons gelatine in 8 tablespoons water. Bring 2 pints clarified beef stock to boil and add gelatine to dissolve. Season with 1 teaspoon Worcestershire sauce and 2 tablespoons lemon juice or dry white wine. Cool and chill until set. Break up with fork and serve with garnish of choice.
Serves 6

JELLIED MADRILENE

Combine 2-1/2 pints rich chicken or veal stock with 3/4 pint tomato purée. Simmer 30 minutes and add 2 tablespoons gelatine softened in 8 tablespoons water. Heat to dissolve gelatine, cool and chill until set.
Serves 8.

TURKEY BROTH WITH AVOCADO

2-1/2 pints rich turkey broth
2 avocados, diced, sliced or cut in rings
lemon juice

Heat broth to boiling and adjust seasonings to taste. Sprinkle avocados with lemon juice and just before serving add to hot broth. Garnish with finely chopped parsley.
Serves 6.
You may lace with dry sherry.

CONSOMMÉ PRINCESSE

2-1/2 pints chicken, veal, and/or beef stock

6—8 tablespoons each fresh green peas or asparagus tips, and shredded cooked chicken

4 tablespoons grated Parmesan cheese
finely chopped chervil

Bring stock to boil and adjust seasonings to taste. Add peas or asparagus and cook until just tender-crisp. Reheat with chicken and sprinkle with cheese and finely chopped chervil.
Serves 6

STRACCIATELLA

2-1/2 pints rich beef broth or consommé

6 eggs, beaten
4 ounces grated Parmesan cheese
1/2 teaspoon salt
1/4 teaspoon black pepper
1 tablespoon finely chopped flat leaf parsley

finely chopped chives

Bring broth or consommé to boil and adjust seasonings to taste.
Beat eggs, cheese, salt, pepper and parsley. Gradually pour into boiling soup, stirring with a fork to make ribbons of egg. Cook a few minutes to set eggs. Serve garnished with finely chopped chives.
Serves 6
Or add cooked soup pasta and garnish with tomato dice.

CHICKEN BROTH WITH MUSHROOMS

2-1/2 pints chicken broth

6 ounces diced cooked chicken
6—8 tablespoons sliced mushrooms, sautéed in
  1 tablespoon butter
1/4 pound cooked thin noodles or cooked rice
lemon juice

finely chopped chervil or watercress

Bring broth to boil and adjust seasonings to taste. Add chicken, mushrooms, and noodles or rice. Reheat and season with lemon juice. Garnish with finely chopped chervil or watercress.
Serves 6

CLEAR CELERY SOUP

2-1/2 pints chicken stock
3 stalks celery and some leaves, chopped
1 small leek, white part only, chopped
2 large tomatoes, peeled and diced
3 tablespoons butter

finely chopped celery leaves

Steam vegetables in butter, covered, 20 minutes.
Add stock and cook 30 minutes.
Strain, adjust seasonings and garnish with finely chopped celery leaves.
Serves 6

CHICKEN BROTH WITH GIBLETS

2-1/2 pints chicken stock
4 tablespoons chopped mushroom stems
6—8 tablespoons each chopped onion, carrot, celery
  and leaves
4 tablespoons diced core of cauliflower
2 shredded cabbage leaves
1 bay leaf
6 parsley sprigs

giblets from 2 or 3 chickens

finely chopped parsley

Simmer stock, mushroom stems, vegetables, bay leaf and parsley 1 hour. Strain. Bring to boil.
Slice hearts and gizzards and add to boiling stock; cook 15 minutes.
Halve the livers, add to stock and cook 5 minutes.
Sprinkle with finely chopped parsley.
Serves 6

GAME BROTH

2-1/2 pints clarified game stock
salt
pepper
thyme
12 chicken or game balls, cooked (see page 178)

finely chopped chervil
Parmesan croutons

6 tablespoons dry red wine

Heat stock and adjust seasonings.
Add chicken or game balls and garnish with finely chopped chervil and Parmesan croutons.
Serve with a tablespoon of red wine in each bowl.
Serves 6

TOMATO BOUILLON

1-1/2 pints chicken stock
1 14-ounce can Italian tomatoes

curry powder
lemon juice
pinch sugar

marrow dumplings (see page 176)

Cook stock and tomatoes 30 minutes. Force through food mill or sieve, reheat and season to taste.
Serve hot with marrow dumplings.
Serves 6
Or omit curry, lemon juice and dumplings. Add dry sherry or dry vermouth and serve icy cold.

CLEAR OXTAIL BROTH

2-1/2 pounds oxtails, cut up
1/4 pound diced ham
3 stalks celery, chopped
2 large carrots, chopped
1 small onion, chopped
6—8 tablespoons chopped turnip
4 tablespoons chopped leek
3 tablespoons butter

2-1/2 pints water
2 savory sprigs
1 tarragon sprig
2 thyme sprigs
4 parsley sprigs
3 tablespoons ketchup
scant 1/2 pint port wine
1 teaspoon salt
1/2 teaspoon pepper

1-1/2 tablespoons butter
1 tablespoon flour

6 ounces slivered meat from oxtails

finely chopped parsley

Sauté oxtails, ham and vegetables in butter over high heat, stirring often, until golden.
Add water, herbs, ketchup, port, salt and pepper.
Cover, bring to boil and cook 3 hours until oxtails are tender. Skim surface scum whenever necessary.
Strain, reserving oxtails. Cool, chill and defat.
Melt butter until bubbly, sprinkle with flour and cook and stir 3 minutes. Gradually add oxtail stock; cook and stir until smooth.
Adjust flavors with salt, pepper, ketchup and port. Reheat with meat and garnish with lots of finely chopped parsley.
Serves 6

VEGETABLE CONSOMMÉ

2 medium-sized onions, finely chopped
2 small leeks, finely chopped
6—8 tablespoons chopped celeriac
6—8 tablespoons chopped turnip and/or swede
2 large carrots, chopped
1/4 pound cabbage, shredded
3 tablespoons butter

scant 3 pints water
1 teaspoon salt
3 peppercorns
2 sprigs thyme
6 parsley sprigs
2 tablespoons fresh basil

finely chopped fresh herbs

Sauté vegetables in butter, stirring, 10 minutes. Add water and seasonings, cover, bring to boil and simmer 2 hours.
Strain, adjust seasonings to taste and serve hot or cold with finely chopped fresh herbs.
Serves 6

DOUBLE MUSHROOM CONSOMMÉ

2-1/2 pints rich chicken, beef and/or veal stock
2 large dried mushrooms, soaked in water to cover
  with a pinch of sugar, until softened
3 spring onions and tops, slivered
1/2 pound mushrooms, finely chopped

lemon juice
dry white wine
salt
pepper

raw mushrooms for garnish
lemon juice

Dice dried mushrooms and combine with stock, spring onions and fresh mushrooms. Cover, bring to boil and simmer 45 minutes. Strain, pushing as much pulp through sieve as possible.
Season with lemon juice, wine, salt and pepper and serve with thinly sliced raw mushrooms tossed with lemon juice.
Serves 6

CONSOMMÉ PRINTANIER

2-1/2 pints rich consommé of choice

3 tablespoons each turnips and carrots, cut in julienne strips, blanched and drained

6—8 tablespoons cooked peas
6—8 tablespoons cooked French beans, cut diagonally in small pieces

finely chopped chervil
lemon slices

Bring consommé to boil, add turnips and carrots and cook until almost done. Add peas and beans and reheat. Vegetables should be tender-crisp.
Sprinkle with finely chopped chervil and serve with lemon slices.
Serves 6
May substitute asparagus tips and/or small kidney or haricot beans for peas and French beans.

POACHED EGG CONSOMMÉ OR BROTH.

2-1/2 pints rich consommé or broth of choice

6 whole eggs

finely chopped chives, parsley or chervil
toast or croutons

Bring stock to boil and adjust seasonings. Break an egg into 6 heated bowls and pour hot soup over to poach lightly. Garnish with finely chopped chives, parsley or chervil and serve with toast or croutons. Eggs can be poached first if firmer eggs are desired.
Serves 6

CONSOMMÉ BRUNOISE

2-1/2 pints rich stock of choice

4 tablespoons each finely shredded carrots, leeks and turnips
4 tablespoons each thinly sliced celery and cauliflower

2 tablespoons butter

4 tablespoons finely chopped parsley

lemon peel

Sauté vegetables in butter until just tender-crisp. Add to heated stock, stir in parsley and serve with a garnish of fine strips of lemon peel.
Serves 6

CELERIAC CONSOMMÉ

2-1/2 pints consommé of choice

lemon juice
2—2-1/2 pounds celeriac, peeled and sliced

finely chopped parsley

Reserve 3 slices of celeriac; cut them into julienne strips and soak them in cold water and lemon juice.
Cook consommé and remaining celeriac slices for 1 hour, strain and bring to boil. Add drained julienne strips and cook until they are just tender-crisp.
Sprinkle with finely chopped parsley.
Serves 6

SPAETZLE-SUPPE

2-1/2 pints stock of choice

Spaetzle:

1 egg, beaten
6–8 tablespoons milk
1 teaspoon melted butter
1/2 teaspoon salt
5 tablespoons flour
mixed fresh herbs: chervil, chives, parsley, summer savory

Combine egg, milk, butter and salt. Beat in flour to make a very soft dough. Force dough through a colander or slotted spoon into gently boiling stock. Cook 3 minutes until spaetzle rise to top. Simmer 3 more minutes.
Sprinkle with mixed fresh herbs.
Serves 6

BROTH WITH MACARONI

2-1/2 pints rich broth
2 ounces small shell macaroni
2 eggs, beaten with tiny bits of meat, liver, chicken or game and 1 teaspoon finely chopped parsley

Bring broth to boil, add macaroni and cook until tender. Gradually drizzle egg mixture into gently boiling broth and cook until set.
Serves 6

BEEF BROTH WITH DUMPLINGS

2 pints beef broth
scant 1/2 pint dry red wine
1/2 teaspoon sugar
1/2 tablespoon lemon juice

1 recipe dumplings of choice (see pages 175–7)

lemon slices

Heat broth, wine, sugar and lemon juice and adjust flavors to taste.
Add cooked dumplings and serve with lemon slices.
Serves 6
Or omit wine and flavor 2-1/2 pints broth with tarragon and/or oregano. Garnish with tomato dice.

CHICKEN-CLAM BROTH WITH ROYALES

2 pints rich chicken stock
scant 1/2 pint canned clam juice (or fish stock)

1 recipe royales (see page 179)

6 teaspoons dry sherry

finely chopped chives
paprika

Heat stock and clam juice; adjust seasonings to taste.

Divide royales between 6 heated bowls with a teaspoon of sherry in each. Ladle in hot broth and sprinkle with finely chopped chives and paprika.
Serves 6
Or float a curl of spinach leaf in each bowl with a shred of carrot and a tiny strip of lemon peel.

PELMENY BROTH

6 cups rich stock

1 recipe pelmeny (see below)

finely chopped chives
hot mustard
white vinegar
aji oil*

*see glossary

Bring stock to boil. Adjust seasoning. Place cooked pelmeny in bowls and ladle soup over them. Sprinkle with finely chopped chives and serve with hot mustard, white vinegar and aji oil.

PELMENY

Dough:
4 ounces plain flour
1/2 teaspoon salt
2 egg yolks
3—4 tablespoons cold water, to make a stiff dough

Filling:
1 pound minced beef or combination of beef,
  pork and veal
3 tablespoons grated onion
1/2 teaspoon salt
1/4 teaspoon black pepper
2 tablespoons finely chopped mushroom stems
1/2 teaspoon dill

Mix dough ingredients and knead at least 10 minutes until smooth and elastic. Form into a ball and cover with inverted bowl for 1 hour. Roll into a rope 1/2-inch thick and cut off 1-inch pieces. Roll as thin as possible into 2-1/2-inch rounds.

Combine filling ingredients. Put 3/4 teaspoon filling on each round. Fold over to make half-moon shape and crimp edges to seal. Place on floured baking sheets and chill (or freeze) 30 minutes.

Cook in boiling salted water 7 minutes.

Vegetable Soups

"Beautiful soup! Who cares for fish
Game, or any other dish?
Who would not give all else for two
Pennyworth only of beautiful soup?"
                    —Alice in Wonderland

The prosaic dried lentil, bean, and pea soups of the ancients lend themselves to a modern approach, for their bland flavors go well with a number of other ingredients. Potatoes, too, can be the basis of a whole family of soups. People usually think of vegetable soup as colorful green peas, diced carrots, onion rings, or other "fresh" vegetables in clear broth. All kinds of vegetable soups are included here. The old-fashioned approach of soaking dried legumes overnight and then cooking them, and fresh vegetables, too, until completely soft (and usually mushy) is out of date as far as I am concerned. Vegetables should be cooked only enough to make them tender without destroying their crispness or leaching out their flavor, except, of course, when making stock or purées. Even most dried legumes, I think, should retain their shape and identity. Presoaking after washing and picking over need only consist of pouring boiling water over them, boiling them for 2 minutes, then letting them stand, covered, for 2 hours, except in the case of chickpeas; longer soaking in water to cover allows them to swell and absorb liquid for shorter cooking later.

FRESH ARTICHOKE SOUP

1 garlic clove, finely chopped
1 small onion, finely chopped
1 tablespoon olive oil
3-4 artichokes
1-1/4 pints beef or chicken stock
1 tablespoon lemon juice
1/2 tablespoon black peppercorns
1/2 tablespoon oregano

2 tablespoons chopped spring onions, white
  part only
1 garlic clove, finely chopped
1 tablespoon butter

1 can condensed cream of mushroom soup
1/4 pint single cream
1/4 pint milk

1/2 teaspoon each salt and pepper
6—8 tablespoons white wine

Sauté chopped garlic and onion in olive oil in a heavy saucepan. Add artichokes, stock, lemon juice, peppercorns and oregano. Simmer, covered, until artichokes are very tender, adding more water if needed. Remove artichokes, strain and reserve stock.
Scrape edible portion from the artichoke leaves, remove chokes and dice hearts, reserving one heart for garnish.
Sauté spring onions and garlic in butter 3 minutes; purée in blender with artichokes and 1/4 pint of the reserved stock.
Blend soup, cream and milk into pureé; season with salt and pepper. Heat and adjust seasonings. Just before serving add wine and reserved diced artichoke heart. Serves 4—6
Or add 4 tablespoons tomato juice (or to taste) instead of the wine and reheat.

CREAM OF BROCCOLI SOUP

2 - 2-1/2 pounds broccoli
6—8 tablespoons finely chopped onion
4 tablespoons finely chopped green pepper
2 tablespoons butter and/or rendered chicken fat

2 tablespoons flour
2-1/2 pints rich chicken stock
bouquet garni of:
 1 bay leaf
 3 parsley sprigs
 1 thyme sprig
 6 peppercorns

1/4 teaspoon nutmeg or
 1/2 teaspoon curry powder
1/4 teaspoon white pepper

2 - 3 egg yolks
scant 1/4 pint double cream
salt

slivered spring onions
sour cream

Reserve 12 small broccoli flowerets and chop remainder. Sauté broccoli, onion and green pepper in butter and/or fat to brown slightly.
Sprinkle with flour, cook and stir 3 minutes and add stock and bouquet garni. Cook and stir until smooth and slightly thickened. Cover, bring to boil, and simmer 30 minutes until broccoli is soft. Discard bouquet garni.
Purée in blender and force through sieve to remove any stringy particles. Add nutmeg or curry and pepper.
Beat yolks and cream, whisk in 1/4 pint hot soup and return to rest of soup. Reheat; do not boil. Season with salt to taste and serve with slivered spring onions and dollops of sour cream.
Serves 6 - 8
Or omit nutmeg or curry. Add 3 tablespoons tomato paste and mix well. Stir in 4 ounces cooked macaroni, reheat and serve garnished with grated Parmesan cheese.

GREEN PEPPER SOUP

4 small green peppers, finely chopped
1 medium-sized onion, finely chopped
4 tablespoons finely chopped carrot
1 garlic clove, finely chopped
3 slices bacon, finely chopped

1 can (14-ounce) peeled tomatoes, with juices
1-1/2 pints beef and/or chicken stock
1/2 teaspoon salt
1/4 teaspoon black pepper
1/4 teaspoon basil
1 pound minced lean beef

Sauté green peppers, onion, carrot, garlic and bacon until bacon is slightly browned.
Add tomatoes, stock, salt, pepper, basil and meat. Cover, bring to boil, and simmer 45 minutes.
Adjust seasonings to taste.
Serve with garlic French bread.
Serves 6

CREAMY CABBAGE SOUP

2 ounces fat salt pork, finely chopped
2 tablespoons unsalted butter
3 tablespoons finely chopped shallots
1 garlic clove, finely chopped
1 tablespoon flour
2 pints chicken or beef stock
1 pound Savoy cabbage, finely shredded
bouquet garni of:
   1 bay leaf
   2 parsley sprigs
   1 thyme sprig
   6 peppercorns
1/2 pint creamy milk
1/4 pint sour cream
1/8 teaspoon nutmeg
1/4 teaspoon white pepper
1/2 teaspoon salt
2 egg yolks, beaten
1/4 pint double cream
finely chopped parsley
grated Emmenthal cheese

Brown salt pork in butter, remove with slotted spoon and reserve.

Add shallots and garlic to pan and sauté until just golden.

Sprinkle with flour, cook and stir 3 minutes and gradually add stock. Cook and stir until smooth and slightly thickened.

Add creamy milk mixed with sour cream, reheat and simmer 30 minutes. Discard bouquet garni and purée soup in blender.

Add creamy milk mixed with sour cream reheat and season with nutmeg, pepper and salt.

Beat yolks with double cream, whisk in 1/4 pint hot soup and return to rest of soup. Reheat without boiling, and adjust seasonings with salt.

Garnish with reheated salt pork bits, finely chopped parsley and grated Emmenthal cheese.

Serves 6 - 8

Or add tomatoes, or sautéed, finely chopped green pepper, and julienne strips of ham. Top with diced canned red pepper or sprinkle with caraway seeds.

29

CREAM OF CELERY SOUP

4 stalks celery and some tops, chopped
1 medium-sized onion, chopped
1-1/2 pints rich chicken stock

4 stalks celery, thinly sliced on diagonal
6–8 tablespoons chopped green celery leaves
3 tablespoons each butter and flour

1/2 pint milk
1/4 pint double cream
1/8 teaspoon nutmeg
1/4 teaspoon white pepper
1/2 teaspoon celery salt

salt

chiffonade of sorrel (see page 179)

Simmer chopped celery and onion in stock 45 minutes. Strain.
Sauté sliced celery and leaves in butter 5 minutes, sprinkle with flour, cook and stir 3 minutes. Gradually add stock; cook and stir until smooth and slightly thickened.
Cover and simmer 15 minutes.
Add milk, cream and seasonings, and reheat
Adjust seasonings with salt.
Just before serving add chiffonade of sorrel, a very important addition.
Serves 4 - 6
Or add 2 peeled, seeded and diced tomatoes when cooking thickened soup. Garnish with bacon bits or toasted almonds and finely chopped parsley, or top with grated cheese.

CREAM OF CELERIAC SOUP

1/2 pound celeriac, diced
1 small onion, diced
2 tablespoons finely chopped leek
1 teaspoon finely chopped garlic
3 tablespoons butter
1/2 teaspoon dry mustard
1/8 teaspoon sugar

3/4 pint chicken or veal stock

1/4 pint milk
1/4 pint single cream

salt
white pepper
celery salt

lemon juice

2–3 ounces tiny julienne strips of celeriac, cooked in a little stock until tender
paprika
finely chopped parsley

Sauté celeriac, onion, leek and garlic in butter 5 minutes. Sprinkle with mustard and sugar and cook and stir 5 more minutes.
Add stock, cover, bring to boil and simmer until celeriac is tender. Purée in blender, add milk and cream and heat without boiling. Season to taste with salt, pepper, celery salt and lemon juice.
Serve garnished with strips of celeriac and a sprinkling of paprika and finely chopped parsley.
Serves 4
May also be served cold. Chill, adjust seasonings and serve in chilled bowls garnished with tiny lemon peel strips.

CUCUMBER-CELERY MÉLANGE

1 cucumber, peeled, seeded and cut into
 1-inch julienne strips
2 stalks celery, thinly sliced on diagonal
1 leek, white only, finely chopped
bouquet garni of:
 1 sprig thyme
 5 sprigs parsley
 1 bay leaf
 6 peppercorns

1-1/2 tablespoons flour
1-1/2 pints rich chicken stock
4 tablespoons dry white wine

2 cucumbers, peeled, seeded and cut into
 1-inch julienne strips
1/2 teaspoon salt

1 egg yolk, beaten
scant 1/2 pint double cream
1 teaspoon lemon juice
1/4 teaspoon each white pepper and
 celery salt

lemon slices
parsley sprigs

Steam cucumber, celery, leek and bouquet garni in butter, covered, until vegetables are soft.

Sprinkle with flour, cook and stir 3 minutes and gradually add stock and wine. Cook and stir until smooth and slightly thickened. Cover and simmer 10 minutes. Discard bouquet garni.

While soup is simmering, sprinkle cucumbers with salt and let stand in colander to drain. Rinse, drain and dry on paper towels. Add to soup and cook 4 minutes.

Beat yolk and cream, whisk in 1/4 pint hot soup and return to rest of soup. Reheat but do not boil. Season and adjust to taste. Serve with lemon slices and tiny parsley sprigs.

Serves 4

Or add a chiffonade of sorrel (see page 179) in place of the lemon slices and serve with lemon croutons.

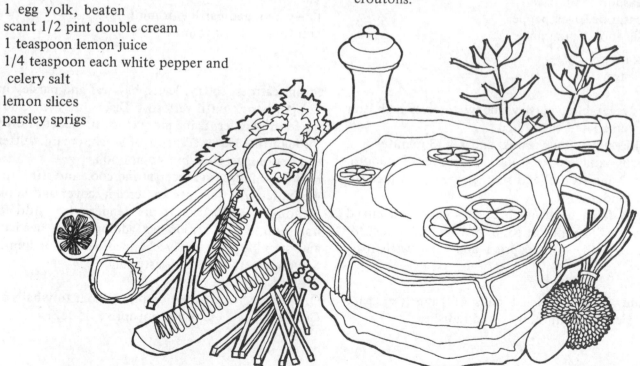

GREEN SOUP

2 ounces each finely chopped sorrel, spinach,
  dandelion greens, kale, Swiss chard or
  any green leafy vegetable or combination to
  make about 6 ounces in all
1 small stalk celery sliced thinly on diagonal
6—8 tablespoons finely chopped spring onions
  and tops
4 tablespoons each finely chopped leeks,
  parsley and watercress
3 tablespoons butter

1 tablespoon flour
1-1/2 pints rich game stock, or chicken stock or
  combination

scant 1/2 pint sour cream

1/2 teaspoon salt
1/4 teaspoon black pepper
1 tablespoon lemon juice

paprika
toast fingers

Sauté vegetables, parsley and watercress in butter
until well coated and wilted.
Sprinkle with flour, cook and stir 3 minutes and
gradually add stock. Cook and stir until smooth.
Cover, bring to boil and simmer gently until celery
is just tender-crisp.
Remove from heat and beat in sour cream mixed
first with 1/4 pint hot soup. Season and adjust to
taste. Sprinkle with paprika and serve with toast
fingers.
Serves 6
Or add little forcemeat balls of game (see page
178). Garnish with thinly sliced radishes.

CARROT PURÉE

1-1/2 pounds carrots, sliced
1 large stalk celery, chopped
6 small leeks with little green, chopped
1/2-inch piece bay leaf
6 parsley sprigs
2-1/2 pints rich chicken stock

scant 1/2 pint double cream
3 tablespoons butter
1/8 teaspoon nutmeg
1/4 teaspoon white pepper
1/4 teaspoon grated lemon rind

1/2 teaspoon brown sugar
6—8 tablespoons shredded carrot
4 tablespoons double cream

salt
finely chopped parsley or mint
croutons or toast rounds

Steam carrots, celery, leeks, bay leaf and parsley in
1/2 pint stock until very soft. Discard bay leaf and
purée in blender, using more stock if needed. Force
through fine sieve, add rest of stock, cream, butter
and seasonings. Heat but do not boil.
Melt brown sugar in saucepan and cook and stir 3 to
4 minutes. Add carrots and cream, cover and cook
10 minutes until carrots are tender-crisp. Add to
hot soup, adjust seasonings, adding salt as needed,
and sprinkle with finely chopped parsley or mint.
Serve with croutons or toast rounds.
Serves 6
Or sprinkle with grated onion, or float tiny balls of
Gorgonzola cheese rolled in paprika on top.

EMMA'S MUSHROOM SOUP

1 pound leg of beef, cut into 1-inch cubes
1 teaspoon salt
1-3/4 pints water
1 small onion, finely chopped
4 ounces butter
1 pound fresh mushrooms, finely chopped
2-1/2 tablespoons flour
1/4 pint milk
1/4 pint single cream

salt

paprika
finely chopped parsley

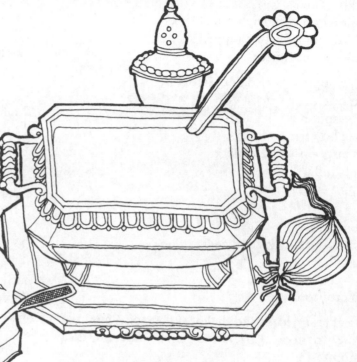

For years Emma ruled the kitchen of a family who ate well, indeed. Now, years later her original recipe can still hold its own against those of famous chefs.

Sprinkle meat with salt, add cold water and let stand 1/2 hour. Cover, bring to slow boil, and simmer gently until meat is tender. Remove meat and reserve for another use or discard. Do not strain as the flavor of the "curds" that have formed enhances the soup.

Sauté onion in butter until soft but not brown. Add mushrooms, sauté and stir 5 minutes; sprinkle with flour, cook and stir 3 minutes, and gradually add broth. Cook and stir until slightly thickened.

Add milk and cream and reheat; do not boil. Season with salt and serve sprinkled with paprika and finely chopped parsley.

Serves 4 - 6

Or garnish with dollops of whipped cream.

CREAMY CHICORY SOUP

1-1/4 pounds chicory or Belgian endive,
  thickly sliced
4 tablespoons finely chopped leeks
2 tablespoons finely chopped shallots
3 tablespoons butter

1 large potato, peeled and diced
piece of chicken stock cube
1/4 teaspoon mixed herbs
1 teaspoon lemon juice
1/4 teaspoon white pepper
2 pints milk
1/2 pint single cream

salt
lemon juice
1 ounce butter, finely diced
paprika
finely chopped parsley
herb croutons

Sauté chicory, leeks and shallots in butter 3 minutes, stirring to coat. Cover and cook over low heat 10 minutes.

Add potato, seasonings and milk; cover, bring to gentle boil and simmer 10 minutes or until potatoes are just soft.

Add cream, reheat, adjust seasonings with salt and lemon juice, and swirl in diced butter.

Sprinkle with paprika and finely chopped parsley and serve with herb croutons.

Serves 6 - 8

CAULIFLOWER SOUP WITH CHEESE

1 large cauliflower, divided into flowerets
1-1/2 pints chicken stock
1 teaspoon soy sauce
1/2 teaspoon each summer savory, paprika and
  garlic powder
1/4 teaspoon black pepper

2 tablespoons butter
2 tablespoons flour
1/2 pint evaporated milk
4 tablespoons freshly grated Parmesan cheese

2 egg yolks, beaten
3 tablespoons lemon juice

Reserve 1/2 cup tiny flowerets for garnish. Cook remainder in stock with soy sauce, savory, paprika, garlic powder and pepper until cauliflower is soft. Purée in blender.

Melt butter until bubbly, add flour, and cook and stir 3 minutes. Gradually add milk; cook and stir until thickened and add purée and cheese. Reheat to melt cheese.

Beat eggs with lemon juice, whisk in 1/4 pint hot soup and return to rest of soup. Reheat; do not boil. Dilute with a little more stock or milk if necessary.

Garnish with reserved raw flowerets and extra cheese.

Serves 6

SPINACH SOUP

1 pound fresh spinach, chopped
2 tablespoons finely chopped spring onions
1 garlic clove, finely chopped
3 tablespoons butter

1/8 teaspoon nutmeg
2 pints chicken, beef or veal stock

1/4 pint single cream
1/4 pint milk
pinch sugar
1/2 teaspoon salt
1/4 teaspoon white pepper
pinch finely grated lemon peel
1 ounce butter, finely diced

sieved hard-boiled eggs
paprika

Sauté spinach, spring onions and garlic in butter, stirring, until spinach is wilted.
Add nutmeg and stock, cover, bring to boil and simmer 20 minutes. Purée in blender.
Add cream, milk and seasonings, heat and adjust to taste. Swirl in diced butter and sprinkle with sieved hard-boiled eggs and paprika.
Serves 6
Or halve 3 small hard-boiled eggs, remove yolks and mash them with 1-1/2 teaspoons softened butter. Form balls and arrange in white halves, garnish with a tiny parsley sprig, and float on hot soup.

CHERVIL SOUP

4 tablespoons butter
5 tablespoons flour
2-1/2 pints rich veal stock

6—8 tablespoons finely chopped chervil, firmly packed with only tender stems

2 - 3 egg yolks, beaten

1/4 teaspoon white pepper
1/2 teaspoon salt

finely chopped chervil

Melt butter until bubbly, add flour, cook and stir 3 minutes. Do not brown. Gradually add stock, cook and stir until smooth and slightly thickened. Continue cooking, stirring occasionally, 30 minutes. Add chervil, bring back to boil and cook 1 minute. Beat yolks and 1/4 pint hot soup; return to rest of soup and heat without boiling. Adjust seasonings to taste with pepper and salt and serve with extra finely chopped chervil.
Serves 6
Or top with finely shredded crisp lettuce.

Potato Soups

HOT POTATO SOUP

6 small leeks, white and some green, finely chopped
4 tablespoons finely chopped onion
1 large garlic clove, finely chopped
3 tablespoons finely chopped carrot
4 tablespoons butter and/or rendered chicken fat

1-1/2 pints chicken stock
1/2 pound potatoes, peeled and diced

1/4 pint double cream

salt
white pepper
celery salt

Sauté leeks, onion, garlic and carrot in butter and/or fat until leeks are soft. Do not brown.
Add stock and potatoes, cover, bring to boil and simmer until potatoes are tender. Purée in blender. Add cream, reheat but do not boil, and season to taste with salt, pepper and celery salt. If too thick, thin with more stock or with creamy milk.
Serves 6
Or just before serving add 3 tablespoons dry vermouth or dry sherry. Or sprinkle with caraway seeds.

CARROT-POTATO SOUP

1 recipe hot potato soup *without cream*
2 large carrots, diced
4 tablespoons diced celery
3 tablespoons butter
1/2 teaspoon marjoram
pinch sugar
6–8 tablespoons shredded carrot

1/4 pint single cream
1/4 pint milk

salt ,
pepper
marjoram

finely chopped parsley

Sauté carrots and celery in butter until soft, sprinkling with marjoram and sugar as they are cooking. Purée in blender with some of the potato soup, combine with rest of soup, add shredded carrots and simmer 5 minutes.
Reheat with cream and adjust seasonings to taste with salt, pepper and marjoram. Sprinkle with lots of finely chopped parsley.
Serves 6
Or add 1/4 pint double cream, chill and garnish with raw shredded carrots and finely chopped parsley.

CUCUMBER-POTATO SOUP

1 recipe hot potato soup *without cream*

1 large cucumber, peeled, seeded and grated
3 tablespoons grated onion

1/4 pint single cream
1/4 pint milk

salt
white pepper
celery salt
lemon juice
finely chopped fresh dill, slivered spring onions

Combine soup, cucumber and onion; simmer 10 minutes.
Reheat with cream and milk. Do not boil.
Adjust seasonings to taste with salt, pepper, celery salt and a squeeze of lemon juice.
Sprinkle with finely chopped fresh dill or slivered spring onions.
Serves 6
Or add 1/4 pint double cream, chill and garnish with mint and sour cream.

PEA-POTATO SOUP

1 recipe hot potato soup *without cream*

10–12 ounces frozen petits pois, thawed
4 tablespoons finely chopped celery
3 tablespoons butter
1/4 pint single cream
1/4 pint milk

salt
white pepper
summer savory
1 ounce butter, finely diced
paprika

Sauté half of the peas and the celery in butter until celery is soft.
Purée in blender with some of the soup; combine with rest of soup, rest of peas and the cream and milk. Simmer 5 minutes.
Adjust seasonings with salt, pepper and savory, swirl in diced butter and sprinkle with paprika.
Serves 6
Or omit diced butter. Add 1/4 pint double cream, chill and serve with mint.

BROCCOLI-POTATO SOUP

1 recipe hot potato soup *without cream*
1/4 pound broccoli, cooked and chopped
1-1/2 tablespoons grated onion
1/4 pint single cream
1/4 pint milk
finely chopped fresh dill or tiny, raw broccoli
 flowerets

Simmer potato soup, broccoli and onion 10 minutes to blend flavors. Purée in blender.
Reheat with cream and milk and adjust seasonings to
taste.
Garnish with finely chopped fresh dill of tiny raw
broccoli flowerets.
Serves 6
Or add 1/4 pint double cream and chill. Serve
garnished with tiny shrimps or prawns.

PARLSEY-POTATO SOUP

1 recipe hot potato soup *without cream*
4 tablespoons diced celery
1 bunch parsley (4–5 ounces)
3 tablespoons butter

1/4 pint single cream
1/4 pint milk

salt
white pepper

lemon croutons

Remove stems from parsley. Chop finely, reserving
the sprigs. Sauté celery and stems in butter until
celery is soft. Purée in blender with some of the
potato soup, combine with rest of soup, cream, milk
and reserved parsley sprigs, and simmer 5 minutes.

Adjust seasonings to taste with salt and pepper.
Serve with lemon croutons.
Serves 6
Or add 1/4 pint double cream, chill and serve with a
sprinkling of paprika.

WATERCRESS-POTATO

1 recipe hot potato soup *without cream*
4 tablespoons diced celery
1 bunch watercress (about 4 ounces)
3 tablespoons butter

1/4 pint single cream
1/4 pint milk

salt
white pepper

garlic croutons

Sauté celery and the watercress stems, finely
chopped, until celery is tender. Purée in blender with
a little of the soup and combine with rest of soup,
cream, milk and the watercress leaves. Simmer
5 minutes, adjust seasonings with salt and pepper,
and serve with lots of garlic croutons.
Serves 6
Or add 1/4 pint double cream, chill and serve with
extra watercress.

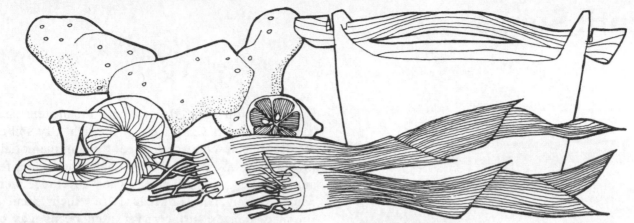

SORREL-POTATO SOUP

1 recipe hot potato soup *without cream*

4–6 ounces sorrel, shredded
1 tablespoon butter and/or rendered chicken fat
pinch dried mixed herbs

1/4 pint single cream
generous 1/4 pint milk

2 egg yolks, beaten

salt
pepper
paprika

Sauté sorrel in butter and/or fat 10 minutes, stirring occasionally. Sprinkle with herbs while cooking. Combine with soup and heat. Beat cream, milk and egg yolks, whisk in 1/4 pint hot soup and return to rest of soup. Adjust seasonings to taste with salt and pepper.
Dust with paprika.
Serves 6
Or add 1/4 pint double cream, chill and garnish with chervil.

MUSHROOM-POTATO SOUP

1 recipe hot potato soup *without cream*

4 ounces mushrooms, finely chopped
4 tablespoons each finely chopped celery and
 spring onions
3 tablespoons butter
1/4 teaspoon garlic powder
1/2 teaspoon lemon juice
dash oregano

1/4 pint single cream
1/4 pint milk
salt
black pepper

paprika
finely chopped fresh dill or parsley

Sauté mushrooms, celery and spring onions in butter until soft, sprinkling with seasonings as they cook. Purée in blender with some of the soup, combine with rest of soup, add cream and milk and heat. Adjust seasonings to taste with salt and pepper. Sprinkle with paprika and minced dill or parsley.
Serves 6
Or add 1/2 pint double cream, chill and garnish with dollops of sour cream and thinly sliced raw mushrooms that have been tossed with lemon juice.

Lentil Soups

Lentils, distinct in flavor, rich in protein and carbohydrates have thrived in the light dry soil of Mediterranean countries since time immemorial, providing soups and cereal for man, and fodder for animals. Magnifying lenses, when invented, were named after lentils because of their similar, rounded, convex surfaces. Peas and beans may be more popular as table food, but lentils will always retain their importance as an ingredient of soup.

LENTIL SOUP

1 carrot, diced
1 onion, diced
1 stalk celery, chopped
1 28-ounce can tomatoes
6 ounces brown lentils
2-1/2 pints water
1 large ham hock

salt
pepper

Purée carrot, onion and celery in blender with a little juice from tomatoes.
Combine with lentils, water and ham hock; cover, bring to boil and simmer 3 hours. Remove ham hock and cut meat into strips. Add to soup, reheat and adjust seasonings with salt and pepper to taste.
Serves 6
Or add diced potatoes or pasta last 10 minutes of cooking.

BROWN LENTIL AND POTATO SOUP

4 slices lean bacon, finely chopped
6—8 tablespoons each diced carrots and onions
2 small stalks celery, diced
1 garlic clove, finely chopped
2 tablespoons diced green pepper

6 ounces brown lentils

3/4 pint water
1-1/4 pints beef or lamb stock
4 tablespoons tomato paste
bouquet garni of:
  3 cloves
  1 bay leaf
  3 parsley sprigs
  1 thyme sprig
1/2 teaspoon salt
1/4 teaspoon black pepper

1/2 pound potatoes, peeled and diced

1-1/2 tablespoons red-wine vinegar
salt and pepper
slivered spring onions

Sauté bacon, carrots, onion, celery, garlic and green pepper until golden.
Combine with lentils, water, stock, tomato paste, bouquet garni, salt and pepper. Cover, bring to boil and simmer 1-1/2 hours.
Add potatoes, bring back to boil and cook 15 minutes. Remove bouquet garni.
Season with vinegar and adjust with salt and pepper. Sprinkle with lots of slivered spring onions.
Serves 6 - 8
Or add cooked spinach and cooked sliced continental-style sausages. Season with allspice.

BROWN LENTIL SOUP WITH SAUSAGE

1/2 pound brown lentils
1-1/2 pints water
1/4 pound salt pork, diced
6—8 tablepoons each diced carrot, onion and celery
bouquet garni of:
  1/2 orange
  3 parsley sprigs
  1 bay leaf
  1 sprig thyme
1/2 teaspoon salt
1/2 teaspoon black pepper
2 tablespoons butter
1-1/2 tablespoons rice flour

beef stock (optional)
dry sherry
sour cream
1/2 pound cooked garlic sausage, sliced

Combine lentils, water, salt pork, vegetables, bouquet garni, salt and pepper. Cover, bring to boil and simmer 1-1/2 hours or until lentils are tender. Discard bouquet garni.
Melt butter until bubbly, stir in rice flour, and cook and stir 3 minutes. Gradually add soup; cook and stir until slightly thickened.
Thin with beef stock if thinner soup is desired. Serve each portion with 1/2 tablespoon dry sherry, 1 teaspoon sour cream and some sliced sausage.
Serves 4 - 6
Or sprinkle with paprika and finely chopped parsley.

LENTIL SOUP WITH FRESH PINEAPPLE

6 ounces brown lentils
1-1/2 pints beef stock
3 tablespoons grated onion
3 garlic cloves, crushed

2 large slices *fresh* pineapple, cut up

1 can (10-1/2-ounce) condensed beef consommé

sour cream

This is not a pretty soup, but the combination of flavors is unusual and surprisingly good.

Combine lentils, stock, onion and garlic. Cover, bring to boil and simmer 1 to 1-1/2 hours until lentils are almost tender.
Add pineapple and cook 10 minutes.
Add consommé, heat and serve with dollops of sour cream.
Serves 4 - 6

MASUR LENTIL SOUP WITH WINE

6 ounces red lentils

4 tablespoons finely chopped bacon or salt pork
6—8 tablespoons finely chopped onion
4 tablespoons chopped carrot
5 tablespoons chopped celery
2 tablespoons chopped parsley
1 garlic clove, finely chopped
1/4 teaspoon each oregano and savory
1/2 teaspoon salt
1/4 teaspoon pepper

3/4 pint beef stock
1 10-1/2-ounce can condensed beef consommé
generous 1/4 pint tomato juice
1 - 2 tablespoons lemon juice

2 tablespoons dry red wine

lemon slices
finely chopped chives

Sauté bacon or pork, vegetables, herbs and seasonings until bacon or salt pork is browned.
Add lentils, stock and consommé, cover, bring to boil and simmer until lentils are soft.
Purée in blender, reheat with tomato juice and add lemon juice. Adjust seasonings to taste.
Just before serving add wine and serve garnished with lemon slices and finely chopped chives.
Serves 4 - 6
Or add 6 to 8 tablespoons finely chopped cooked spinach and sliced hard-boiled eggs.

GARBANZO

2 cups (about 6 ounces) chickpeas, soaked in
 3 cups water overnight

1 medium-sized onion, finely chopped
1 small leek, finely chopped
4 tablespoons finely chopped green pepper
2 teaspoons finely chopped garlic
4 tablespoons olive oil

1-1/2 pints rich beef stock
1 small ham hock
1 teaspoon paprika
1/2 teaspoon salt
1/4 teaspoon pepper
1/8 teaspoon powdered saffron or a pinch of
  saffron strands

1/2 pound sausages, sliced and sautéed in
1/2 tablespoon butter

garlic croutons

Sauté onion, leeks, green pepper and garlic in oil
until onion is soft.
Add chickpeas and their liquid, stock, ham hock,
and seasonings. Cover, bring to boil and simmer
until chickpeas are tender, adding water or stock if
needed.
Remove ham hock and cut meat into small dice.
Return diced ham to soup and adjust seasonings to
taste. Add sausage slices and serve with garlic croutons.
Serves 6 - 8
Or add diced potatoes the last 15 minutes of cooking and garnish with finely chopped mint.

WHITE BEAN SOUP

1 medium-sized onion, finely chopped
2 stalks celery with some leaves, chopped
1 small leek, finely chopped
3 tablespoons butter
3/4 pound dried white beans
2-1/2 pints chicken stock
1 small ham hock
1 calf's tongue, blanched and rinsed
bouquet garni of:
  3 parsley sprigs
  1 thyme sprig
  1 bay leaf
  6 peppercorns
1/2 teaspoon salt
1/4 teaspoon white pepper
dash cayenne

1-1/2 ounces butter, finely diced
6—8 tablespoons finely chopped parsley

paprika
horseradish

Sauté onion, celery and leek in butter until onion is soft. Combine with beans, stock, ham hock, tongue, bouquet garni, salt, pepper and cayenne. Cover, bring to boil and simmer 2 hours, or until beans are soft but not mushy.

Discard bouquet garni. Remove ham hock and tongue and cut as much into dice as desired. Return diced meat to soup, heat and adjust seasonings to taste.

Stir in diced butter and parsley, and sprinkle with paprika. Serve with horseradish and rye bread.

Serves 6 - 8

Or add 1/2 pint tomato juice and sliced Polish or garlic sausages, cooked.

PINTO BEAN SOUP

1/2 pound dried pinto beans
1 ham hock
2-1/2 pints pork stock
1 medium-sized onion, chopped
1 stalk celery, chopped
4 tablespoons each chopped leek and carrot
1 garlic clove, finely chopped
3 tablespoons olive oil

1 28-ounce can tomatoes
bouquet garni of:
  2 cloves
  1 bay leaf
  6 peppercorns
  4 parsley sprigs
1 teaspoon salt
1/2 teaspoon black pepper

1 8-ounce can tomato sauce or 1/2 pint thick fresh
 tomato purée
finely chopped fresh coriander

Sauté onion, celery, leek, carrot and garlic in oil until onion is soft. Add beans, ham hock, stock, tomatoes, bouquet garni, salt and pepper. Cover, bring to boil and simmer 3 hours, or until beans are soft but not mushy. Discard bouquet garni.

Remove ham hock, cut meat into strips and reserve. Purée 3/4 pint of soup (with some beans) and return to rest of soup.

Add ham strips and tomato sauce, reheat and adjust seasonings.

Sprinkle with finely chopped fresh coriander.

Serves 6 - 8

Or add a cup of cooked spaghetti or other pasta.

CREAMY WHITE BEAN SOUP

5 ounces small dried white beans
3/4 pint water
1/2 teaspoon salt

1 large onion, thinly sliced
6—8 tablespoons each chopped celery and
  celery leaves
1 large carrot, chopped
6—8 tablespoons finely chopped parsley
2 tablespoons each olive oil and butter

2 pints veal and/or chicken stock
6—8 tablespoons tomato paste
1/2 teaspoon each basil and white pepper

1/4 pint single cream
1/4 pint milk
salt

chiffonade of sorrel and spinach (see page 179)

Cook beans in salted water 1 hour, adding more water if needed.
Sauté vegetables and parsley in oil and butter, covered, 30 minutes. Do not brown.
Add stock, tomato paste, basil, pepper and beans with their liquid. Cover, bring to boil and simmer 1 hour or until beans are tender.
Purée in blender, reheat with cream and adjust seasonings to taste.
Serve with a chiffonade in each bowl.
Serves 6
Or ladle soup into 6 ovenproof bowls; sprinkle each with 2 tablespoons grated sharp Cheddar cheese and grill to melt cheese.

CUBAN BLACK BEAN SOUP

1 pound black beans
3-1/4 pints water
2 tablespoons salt

1 medium-sized onion, finely chopped
2 small green peppers, finely chopped
2 small stalks celery, finely chopped
2 carrots, finely chopped
6 tablespoons olive oil

5 garlic cloves, finely chopped
1/2 tablespoon cumin
1 tablespoon white vinegar
1 teaspoon Maggi

salt
pepper

finely chopped raw onions
sieved hard-boiled egg yolk

Highly seasoned soup that can be served as a main meal with rice.

Simmer beans in salted water until soft.
Sauté onion, pepper, celery and carrots in oil until onions are brown. Add garlic, cumin, vinegar and Maggi. Cook and stir 3 minutes.
Drain a little water from the beans, add to vegetables, and cook slowly, covered, 30 minutes. Combine with beans, adding more water if needed. Reheat and adjust seasonings with salt and pepper. Serve with bowls of finely chopped raw onions (soaked in olive oil and vinegar if desired) and sieved hard-boiled egg yolk.
Serves 8 - 10

Romanic Soups

Of soup and love the first is the best.
—Spanish Proverb

Perhaps the Roman Empire left more than its language as a heritage to France, Spain, Italy and Portugal. These Latin countries are all unsurpassed in the culinary arts, especially in imaginative soup making.

FRENCH ONION SOUP GRATINÉE

4 large mild onions, thinly sliced
1/2 teaspoon sugar
2 ounces butter and/or rendered chicken fat
1 tablespoon olive oil
1 garlic clove, very finely chopped
2 tablespoons flour
1/4 teaspoon dry mustard
4 tablespoons heated cognac
3/4 pint each beef and chicken stock
1 10-1/2-ounce can condensed beef consommé
1/4 teaspoon nutmeg
1/8 teaspoon black pepper
1/2 teaspoon Worcestershire sauce

6—8 tablespoons dry vermouth or dry white wine

6 slices French bread, toasted
6 tablespoons each grated Gruyère and
  Parmesan cheese

Slowly brown onions and sugar in butter and/or fat and oil. Add garlic, cook 3 minutes and sprinkle with flour and mustard. Cook and stir 3 minutes, raise heat and pour cognac over. Ignite and let burn down. Add stocks, consommé, nutmeg, pepper and Worcestershire sauce. Cover, bring to boil and simmer 20 minutes.

Cool and refrigerate overnight to mellow the flavor. Reheat and adjust seasonings to taste. Just before serving add vermouth or wine.

Ladle soup into ovenproof bowls, top with toasted French bread sprinkled with cheese and grill to melt cheese.

Serves 6

Or omit vermouth or white wine and flavor with dry red wine. Sprinkle toasted cheese with parsley and paprika.

French Soups

SOUPE DE COMPIÈGNE

2 medium-sized mild onions, diced
1/8 teaspoon sugar
4 tablespoons butter
1/2 teaspoon dry mustard
generous 3/4 pint lamb stock

1/2 pint milk
1 egg yolk, beaten
1/4 pint double cream

salt
cayenne

slivered pimiento
finely chopped parsley and/or chives

Sauté onions sprinkled with sugar in butter until starting to turn golden. Sprinkle with mustard and cook 2 minutes. Add stock, cover, bring to boil and simmer until onions are soft.

Purée in blender, add milk and heat. Beat egg yolk and cream, whisk in 1/4 pint of hot soup and reheat. Do not boil.

Adjust seasonings to taste with salt and cayenne and serve with a garnish of slivered pimiento and finely chopped parsley and/or chives.

Serves 4

Or add a chiffonade (see page 179) of chicory and sprinkle with paprika.

POTAGE FINES HERBES

2 ounces sorrel, chopped
1 ounce each lettuce, chervil and watercress,
  chopped
1 large leek, chopped
2 garlic cloves, finely chopped
2 teaspoons finely chopped fresh dill
1 tablespoon butter

1/2 tablespoon flour

3/4 pint chicken stock
piece of chicken stock cube
1 teaspoon finely chopped fresh summer savory
1/2 teaspoon finely chopped fresh basil
1 large potato, peeled and diced
1/2 pint milk
4—6 tablespoons double cream

2 egg yolks, beaten
1/4 pint double cream

watercress sprigs

Sauté herbs and vegetables in butter 5 minutes, stirring to coat well.
Sprinkle with flour, cook and stir 3 minutes and gradually add stock. Cook and stir until smooth.
Add stock cube, savory, basil and potato. Cover, bring to boil and cook until potatoes are soft. Purée in blender.
Reheat with milk and cream.
Beat yolks and 1/4 pint double cream, whisk in 1/4 pint hot soup and return to rest of soup. Heat, but do not boil. Adjust seasonings to taste.
Serve with sprigs of watercress.
Serves 4
Serve with a dish of raw tomatoes, cooked peas, carrots, asparagus and/or beans.

AUBERGINE PURÉE

1 (unpeeled) aubergine, diced (3/4-1 pound)
4 tablespoons finely chopped mushrooms
2 tablespoons finely chopped spring onions
 and tops
1 garlic clove, finely chopped
2 tablespoons olive oil

1-1/4 pints lamb stock
pinch sugar
1-1/2 teaspoons tomato paste
4 tablespoons dry red wine

1 tablespoon butter
1 tablespoon flour
1/4 teaspoon sage

6 fluid ounces double cream
salt
pepper

peeled, seeded and diced tomato
yoghurt

Sauté aubergine, mushrooms, spring onions and garlic in oil, covered, 10 minutes. Stir frequently.
Add stock, sugar, tomato paste and wine. Cover, bring to boil and simmer until aubergine is soft.
Force through sieve and push as much pulp through as possible, leaving the skin.
Melt butter until bubbly, sprinkle with flour and sage, cook and stir 3 minutes. Gradually add aubergine stock; cook and stir until smooth and slightly thickened.
Add cream, reheat without boiling and adjust seasonings to taste with more sage, salt and pepper.
Garnish with diced tomato and serve with a bowl of yoghurt.
Serves 4 - 6

SOUPE DE LAITUE

6 ounces lettuce, shredded (cabbage or cos)
1-1/2 pints rich beef stock
3 ounces watercress, chopped

3 tablespoons butter
4 tablespoons finely chopped onion
2 tablespoons finely chopped green pepper
1 garlic clove, finely chopped
1 teaspoon finely chopped fresh tarragon, or
 1/4 teaspoon dried
2 tablespoons finely chopped parsley
1/8 teaspoon nutmeg
1/8 teaspoon white pepper
2 tablespoons rice (optional)
1/4 pint single cream
1/4 pint milk

2 egg yolks, beaten
6 fluid ounces double cream

salt
pepper

herb croutons

In blender chop lettuce a cup or so at a time, using stock if needed for moisture. Add to rest of stock with watercress.

Sauté onion, green pepper, garlic and herbs in butter until soft; add seasonings and combine with stock mixture. Add rice if desired. Cover, bring to boil, and simmer gently 30 minutes.

Add single cream and milk, and heat. Beat yolks into double cream, whisk in 1/4 pint hot soup, beat, and return to rest of soup. Reheat. Do not boil. Adjust seasonings to taste.

Serve with generous portions of herb croutons.

Serves 6

Or add cooked peas, chopped water chestnuts (canned) and finely chopped spring onions. Sprinkle with a little shredded raw lettuce.

MUSHROOM VELOUTÉ

1 pound mushrooms, sliced (save 8 caps, slice and
  sauté in 1 tablespoon butter)
6–8 tablespoons finely chopped onions
4 tablespoons finely chopped celery
1 garlic clove, finely chopped
3 tablespoons butter and/or olive oil
1 teaspoon lemon juice
1/8 teaspoon dry mustard
1/16 teaspoon cayenne pepper
1/2 teaspoon celery salt
2 tablespoons flour
2-1/2 pints chicken or beef stock
3 parsley sprigs
1 thyme sprig or 1/2 teaspoon dried thyme

2 egg yolks, beaten
6 fluid ounces double cream
2 tablespoons butter, softened

salt

paprika
finely chopped chervil

Sauté onions, celery and garlic in butter and/or oil
until soft; add mushrooms and seasonings and cook
until slightly browned. Sprinkle with flour, cook
and stir 3 minutes, and gradually add stock. Cook
and stir until smooth and slightly thickened.

Add parsley and thyme, cover and simmer 30 minutes. Strain.

Add reserved caps, simmer 5 minutes; beat yolks
with cream; whisk in 1/4 pint hot soup and return
to rest of soup. Reheat but do not boil. Swirl in
butter, adjust seasonings and serve with a sprinkling
of paprika and finely chopped chervil.

Serves 6

Or omit the liaison of yolks and cream, add 5
tablespoons dry sherry and 4 tablespoons each
single cream and milk. Pour into ovenproof bowls,
spread with salted whipped cream and slivered
almonds, and grill briefly to brown cream.

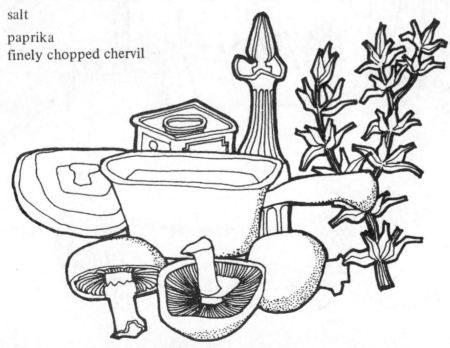

POTAGE PAYSANNE

1-1/2 pints chicken stock
1 beef stock cube
6—8 tablespoons finely chopped leek
 with some green
1 chopped carrot
1 chopped turnip
1 diced potato
4—6 ounces frozen peas
4 cabbage leaves
6 lettuce leaves
6 sprigs each parsley and watercress

6 - 8 large fresh mint leaves
1 tablespoon fresh dill

1/4 pint single cream
1/4 pint milk
2 tablespoons lemon juice
2 tablespoons butter
1/4 teaspoon black pepper
1/2 teaspoon salt

sour cream

Simmer stock, stock cube, vegetables, parsley and watercress until vegetables are soft.
Add mint and dill; purée in blender.
Reheat with cream, milk, lemon juice and butter.
Season with pepper and salt, and adjust to taste.
Serve with dollops of sour cream.
Serves 6
Or garnish with chopped watercress and diced tomato. For a heartier soup add cooked sliced continental-style sausage.
Dry vermouth adds a special zest.

POTAGE DUBARRY

1 large cauliflower, divided into flowerets
2 stalks celery, chopped
1 medium-sized onion, chopped
4 tablespoons chopped carrot
3 tablespoons butter and/or rendered chicken fat

2 tablespoons rice flour
1-1/4 pints chicken or veal stock

1/4 teaspoon each garlic powder and pepper
dash cayenne

1/2 pint milk
1/4 pint double cream

1 teaspoon curry powder
2 teaspoons lemon juice
salt

finely chopped parsley

Reserve 1/2 cup tiny flowerets for garnish. Sauté remainder with celery, onion and carrot in butter and/or fat until well coated and softened.
Sprinkle with flour, cook and stir 3 minutes and gradually add stock. Cook and stir until smooth and slightly thickened.
Season with garlic powder, pepper and cayenne, cover and simmer 30 minutes. Purée in blender, add milk and cream, and heat.
Add curry, lemon juice and salt and adjust to taste.
Garnish with reserved raw cauliflowerets and finely chopped parsley.
Serves 6

POTAGE GERMINY

1/2 pound sorrel, chopped
2 tablespoons butter
2 tablespoons rendered chicken fat

1 tablespoon flour
1-1/2 pints rich chicken stock
1/4 teaspoon white pepper

3 egg yolks, beaten
1/4 pint double cream
1/2 pint milk

salt
lemon juice or dry sherry or Madeira

paprika
finely chopped parsley

Sauté sorrel in butter and fat until limp and discolored.
Sprinkle with flour, stir and cook 3 minutes, and gradually add stock. Cook and stir until smooth and slightly thickened. Season with pepper, cover, bring to boil and simmer 15 to 20 minutes, stirring occasionally. Purée in blender.
Beat egg yolks and cream, whisk in 1/4 pint hot soup and return to rest of soup, together with milk. Reheat without boiling.
Adjust seasonings to taste with salt and lemon juice. Or season with sherry or Madeira. Sprinkle with paprika and finely chopped parsley and serve with toast fingers.
Serves 6
Basil, marjoram and lovage go beautifully with sorrel. If you have them in your herb garden use them.

SORREL BROTH

6 ounces sorrel, finely chopped
2-1/2 pints rich chicken broth

3 eggs, beaten

4 tablespoons dry sherry
finely chopped parsley
herb croutons

Simmer sorrel and broth 15 minutes.
Whisk 1/4 pint hot broth into beaten eggs and return to rest of soup. Reheat without boiling.
Adjust seasonings to taste, add sherry, sprinkle with finely chopped parsley and serve with herb croutons.
Serves 6
Or add finely shredded lettuce and finely chopped chervil to the sorrel.

POTAGE SAINT-CLOUD

2 pounds fresh shelled peas
2-1/2 pints chicken stock
bouquet garni of:
  1/2 onion
  1 garlic clove
  1 sprig thyme
  1 sprig chervil
  4 sprigs parsley
  1/2 teaspoon basil
  2 spring onions and tops, cut up
  1 bay leaf
1 teaspoon turmeric

1/2 teaspoon salt
1/4 teaspoon pepper
1 teaspoon curry powder
1 ounce butter, finely diced

reserved peas
finely chopped chervil

Combine peas, stock, bouquet garni and turmeric; cover, bring to boil and cook 5 minutes until peas are just tender-crisp. Remove 1/2 cup of peas and reserve. Continue cooking remaining peas 30 minutes. Purée in blender.

Season with salt, pepper and curry and adjust to taste. Swirl in diced butter.

Serve with reserved peas and a sprinkling of finely chopped chervil.

Serves 6

Or omit butter and curry. Add 1/2 pint double cream and flavor to taste with dry sherry. Garnish with diced shrimps or prawns.

AMBASSADEURS

Use lamb stock, add a chiffonade (see page 179) of sorrel and a cup of cooked rice, and serve hot.

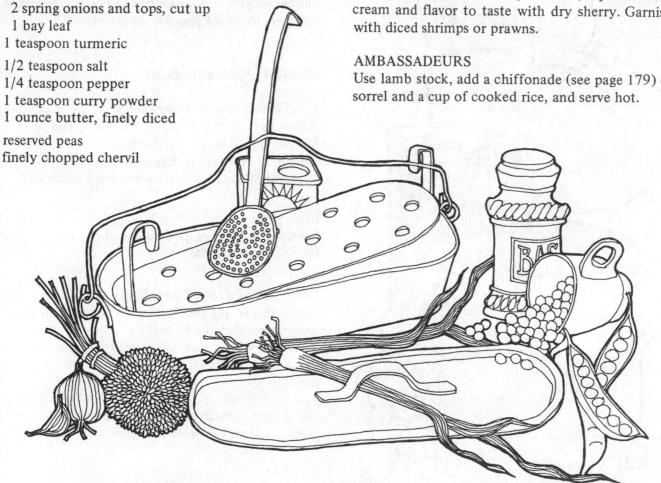

Spanish Soups

According to Jorge Rosell and his wife, former Catalonians who now operate a fascinating grocery import store in San Francisco, gazpacho is served with green tomatoes and is more a salad than a soup. They offer the following six soup ideas as truly representative of Catalonia, where garlic, onion, and pimentón (a sharp paprika) in descending order are the most popular seasonings.

SPANISH PUMPKIN SOUP

2-1/2 pints chicken or beef stock
2 pounds fresh pumpkin, peeled and cubed
4 garlic cloves, finely chopped
2 small onions, finely chopped
4—8 tablespoons finely chopped fresh coriander

salt
black pepper
bread cubes fried in garlic olive oil
fresh coriander sprigs

Combine first five ingredients and cook until pumpkin is soft. Purée in blender, reheat and adjust seasoning with salt and pepper.
Serve hot with bread cubes fried in garlic olive oil, and garnish with extra coriander.
Serves 6 - 8
Flavor of coriander grows stronger if soup is made ahead and reheated. Can be served cold if non-gelatinous stock is used.

SOPA DE JUDIAS BLANCOS

4 garlic cloves
1 quartered onion
1 ham hock
6 ounces dried haricot beans, rinsed and drained
2-1/2 pints water
1/2 teaspoon salt

1 wedge cabbage (1/8 head)
1 whole carrot, halved
1 small stalk celery, halved

garlic croutons

Tie garlic, onion and ham hock in cheesecloth for easy removal.
Combine with beans, water and salt. Cover, bring to boil and simmer 1-1/2 hours or until beans are almost tender.
Tie cabbage, carrot and celery in cheesecloth and add to soup; continue cooking until vegetables are tender, adding water as needed.
Remove vegetables and ham hock; serve with garlic croutons.
Serves 4 - 6
Or add tomatoes if desired. Serve ham, cabbage, carrot and celery on side for heartier meal.

SOPA DE GALLINA

2-1/2 pints rich chicken stock made with extra onion, fresh coriander and lots of garlic

1 cup small pasta shells, cooked, or
 1 cup cooked rice or 1 cup cooked diced potatoes

1/4 teaspoon powdered saffron
salt

freshly ground pepper

Heat stock and pasta, rice or potatoes. Stir in saffron and adjust seasonings with salt.
Pass the peppermill.
Serves 6

SOPA DE AJO

2-1/2 pints water
1 teaspoon salt
20 whole garlic cloves
2 teaspoons olive oil
4 beaten eggs
6 stale French bread slices

freshly ground pepper

Bring water, salt and garlic to boil and simmer 30 minutes. Remove garlic and add olive oil. Bring back to boil and gradually add eggs; let cook gently until eggs are set.
Add bread slices and let them soak up the broth. Serve immediately and pass the peppermill.
For true garlic lovers, add 5 fresh crushed garlic cloves after the whole cloves have been removed.
Serves 6
Or ladle soup into 6 ovenproof bowls. Add a slice of bread fried in olive oil with garlic and onion and top each with a small egg. Bake in a preheated 375°/Mark 5/190°C oven until eggs are set.

ESCUDELLA

3 ounces chick peas, soaked in water to
  cover 8 hours
3 ounces dried haricot beans
2-1/2 pints water
1 8-ounce ham hock
1 4-ounce piece lean pork
1 8-ounce lean short rib of beef

3 garlic cloves, crushed
1 onion, cut in 8ths
1 small whole cabbage, with bottom scored
  1/2 inch deep in 8ths
6 - 8 small whole potatoes

12 - 16 pilotas (see next column)

salt
freshly ground pepper

A garlicky main-meal soup!

Combine chick peas, haricot beans, water, ham
hock, pork and beef rib. Cover, bring to boil and
cook 1-1/4 hours or until beans start to soften; add
water if needed.
Add garlic, onion, cabbage and potatoes; cook at
medium boil 5 minutes.
Add pilotas and cook 10 minutes, or until vegetables
are tender but not mushy.
Adjust seasonings with salt, adding boiling water if
needed to make about 3 pints soup.
Remove cabbage and meat and place on platter to
be served with the soup.
Place 1 potato and 2 pilotas in each bowl and ladle
soup over. Serve with French bread and pass the
peppermill.
Serves 6 - 8

PILOTAS

1/4 pound each minced beef and lean pork
1/2 teaspoon flour
1 garlic clove, crushed
1 tablespoon very finely chopped parsley
1 teaspoon salt

1 beaten egg white

Combine meat, flour, garlic, parsley and salt. With
floured hands roll into 12 or 16 melon shapes.
Roll each one in flour and then in beaten egg white.

SOPA DE ARROZ

3-1/2 ounces raw rice, well washed
1-1/4 pints water or stock
1/2 teaspoon salt
2 - 4 garlic cloves, crushed
2 teaspoons olive oil

For the invalid—a recuperative soup

Bring water or stock to boil with salt and garlic.
Add rice, bring back to boil, cover and simmer
15 minutes until rice is tender. Drizzle oil over,
cover and remove from heat. Let steep 5 minutes
without stirring.
Serves 3 - 4

WINE GAZPACHO

2 pounds tomatoes, peeled, seeded and diced
1 medium-sized onion, finely chopped
2 garlic cloves, crushed
6–8 tablespoons peeled, seeded and diced cucumber
1 3-1/4-ounce can pitted black olives, halved
4 drops Tabasco
1/2 teaspoon salt
1/4 teaspoon black pepper
1 tablespoon paprika
2 tablespoons olive oil
1/8 teaspoon sugar
1/2 pint dry red wine

extra diced vegetables
finely chopped parsley
herb croutons

Combine ingredients and chill.
Adjust seasonings to taste, and serve in chilled bowls. Serve with extra diced vegetables, finely chopped parsley and herb croutons.
Serves 6 - 8

SPICY GAZPACHO

4–5 slices stale French bread, 1/2 inch thick, cubed and soaked in 1-1/4 pints water
4 teaspoons finely chopped garlic
6–8 tablespoons finely chopped onion
4 large tomatoes, peeled and diced
3 tablespoons each olive oil and wine vinegar
1/2 teaspoon salt
1/4 teaspoon black pepper
6 drops Tabasco
1/8 teaspoon cumin

diced green tomato
fresh coriander sprigs

freshly ground pepper

Purée ingredients (except diced green tomato and coriander sprigs) in blender and chill.
Adjust seasonings and serve in chilled bowls; garnish with lots of diced green tomato and sprigs of coriander.
Pass the peppermill.
Serves 4 - 6

SOPA DE ALMENDRAS

1 tablespoon olive oil
1 tablespoon flour
3/4 pint chicken or veal stock

4 ounces blanched almonds, ground
1/8 teaspoon each allspice and nutmeg
1/4 teaspoon thyme
1/4 teaspoon salt

3/4-1 pint milk

4 tablespoons slivered almonds
1/2 teaspoon pimentón or sharp paprika

Heat oil, add flour and cook and stir 3 minutes. Gradually add stock; cook and stir until smooth and slightly thickened.
Add almonds and seasonings; cover, bring to boil and simmer gently 30 minutes.
Strain, forcing as much pulp through sieve as possible. Thin down with milk, heat and adjust seasonings to taste. Garnish with slivered almonds that have been dusted with pimentón or paprika.
Serves 4 - 6
Good before a main course of lamb. Or serve as a luncheon soup with fruit salad and chicken sandwiches.

SEAFOOD GAZPACHO

1-1/2 pounds mixed shellfish such as prawns, shrimps, lobster, crawfish and crab, cooked, shelled and diced or shredded (about 1 pound prepared weight)
1 garlic clove, crushed
4 tablespoons olive oil
3 hard-boiled eggs
1/2 teaspoon dry mustard
4 tablespoons lemon juice
2 pints tomato juice
2 large tomatoes, peeled, seeded and finely chopped
1 large cucumber, peeled, seeded and finely chopped
1/2 teaspoon Worcestershire sauce
3 drops Tabasco
1/2 teaspoon salt
1/4 teaspoon black pepper
1/16 teaspoon compound chili powder

finely chopped parsley and chives
extra diced vegetables
garlic croutons

Mash garlic, oil, egg yolks, and mustard, stir in lemon juice and a cup or so of tomato juice; blend well and add rest of ingredients. Chill thoroughly. Adjust seasonings to taste and serve in chilled bowls sprinkled with finely chopped parsley and chives.
Pass small dishes of extra chopped tomato, cucumber, green pepper, onion and hard-boiled egg white. Have lots of garlic croutons handy.
Serves 6 - 8

MINESTRONE

This Italian classic of vegetables with pasta can be almost anything you wish to make it. With Italian or French bread and a light salad it often makes a full meal, though it needn't be that hearty. Some say never use smoked ham or bacon; others maintain such flavors are essential. The two recipes that follow are flexible and interchangeable. Use whatever is at hand.

MINESTONE WITH HARICOT BEANS

2 ounces dried haricot beans
1 ham hock
1 whole garlic clove
1 small white onion
3/4 pint water

4 tablespoons finely chopped onion
6–8 tablespoons finely chopped leeks,
    white and some green
1 garlic clove, finely chopped
2 tablespoons olive oil

4 tablespoons finely chopped herbs (parsley, basil,
    summer savory, rosemary, oregano, thyme and/
    or sage)

2-1/2 pints chicken, beef or veal stock
3/4 pound vegetables, sliced (carrots, turnips,
    parnsips, green beans, asparagus, peas, curly
    green endive, potatoes)

2 ounces pasta

1 tablespoon tomato paste
1/2 teaspoon salt
1/4 teaspoon pepper
3/4 teaspoon dry mustard

crumbled blue or Gorgonzola cheese

Italian Soups

Combine beans, ham hock, garlic, onion and water. Cover, bring to boil and simmer 1-1/2 to 2 hours until meat is tender, adding water as needed. Remove ham hock and cut meat into small pieces. Discard garlic and onion and set beans and their liquid aside.

Sauté onion, leeks and garlic in oil 5 minutes, add herbs and cook and stir a little longer to coat well. Add stock, bring to boil and add vegetables; cook 10 minutes or less, depending on which vegetables are used. Keep soup boiling, add beans, liquid, ham and pasta. Boil until pasta is tender.

Add tomato paste, salt, pepper and dry mustard. Adjust to taste and serve garnished with crumbled blue cheese or Gorgonzola.

Serves 6 - 8

MINESTRONE WITH BASIL

2 slices bacon, diced
2 medium-sized onions, chopped

1/2 pound Italian or garlic sausages, sliced,
  browned and drained
3-1/4 pints beef stock
2 tablespoons finely chopped fresh basil
6 to 8 tablespoons finely chopped flat leaf
  parsley
1 garlic clove, crushed
1/4 teaspoon each cayenne pepper and
  black pepper
1 teaspoon salt
1 pound potatoes, peeled and diced

2 ounces soup pasta
1/2 pound fresh spinach leaves,
  shredded if large

croutons
grated Parmesan cheese

Sauté bacon and onion until golden. Add sausage,
stock, basil, parsley, garlic, cayenne and pepper, salt
and potatoes. Cover, bring to boil and cook 10 minutes.
Add soup pasta and cook 6 minutes. Add spinach,
bring back to boil and boil just long enough to cook
the spinach. Adjust seasonings to taste.
Serve with croutons and grated Parmesan cheese.
Serves 8 - 10

ZUPPA MARITATA

4 tablespoons finely chopped spring onions
  and tops
2 ounces mushrooms, finely chopped
1 tablespoon olive oil
dash cayenne
1/4 teaspoon each salt and oregano
1 teaspoon lemon juice
2-1/2 pints rich chicken stock made with extra
  oregano and garlic

1/4 pound broken vermicelli

1 recipe cooked chicken balls (see page 178) or
  1/2 pound cooked chicken, diced

1/4 pint single cream
1/4 pint milk
6 tablespoons grated Parmesan cheese

salt
pepper
oregano

paprika
finely chopped flat leaf parsley
grated Parmesan cheese

Sauté spring onions and mushrooms in oil until soft.
sprinkling with cayenne, salt, oregano and lemon
juice while cooking.
Add stock, bring to boil and stir in vermicelli; cook
7 minutes after the soup comes back to a boil.
Reheat with chicken balls or diced chicken.
Beat eggs and cream, whisk in 1/4 pint of hot soup
and return to rest of soup, together with milk. Heat
but do not boil.

Add Parmesan cheese and adjust seasonings to taste
with salt, pepper and oregano.
Sprinkle with paprika and finely chopped parsley
and serve with extra Parmesan cheese.
Serves 6

ITALIAN ENDIVE SOUP WITH MEATBALLS

1 pound marrow bones, sawed into 3-inch pieces
6 peppercorns
3 parsley sprigs
1 bay leaf
2-1/2 pints beef stock
1 teaspoon salt
2 tablespoons tomato paste

4 ounces each diced onion, celery and carrot
1 large potato, peeled and diced

1 recipe Italian meatballs (see next column)
3/4 pound curly green endive, shredded

finely chopped parsley
grated Parmesan cheese

Combine bones, peppercorns, parsley, bay leaf, stock, salt and tomato paste. Cover, bring to boil and simmer 1 hour. Strain, cool, chill and defat.
Bring soup back to boil, add onion, celery and carrots and cook 10 minutes. Add potatoes and cook 5 more minutes.
Add meatballs and endive and cook 10 minutes. Adjust seasonings.
Sprinkle with finely chopped parsley and serve with more grated Parmesan.
Serves 6 - 8

ITALIAN MEATBALLS

6 ounces lean minced beef
1 egg
1 garlic clove, crushed
3 tablespoons finely chopped flat leaf parsley
1/2 teaspoon salt
1/4 teaspoon each pepper and oregano
1/2 - 1 teaspoon lemon juice
3 tablespoons grated Parmesan cheese

Mix ingredients, chill and form into small balls.

ZUPPA ALLA VERMICELLI (WITH PILOU)

1/2 pound vermicelli, broken
2 tablespoons each butter and olive oil

6—8 tablespoons finely chopped onion
1 garlic clove, finely chopped

1/2 pound canned tomatoes, or fresh tomatoes,
  peeled, seeded and finely chopped

3-1/4 pints rich beef or chicken stock
6—8 tablespoons finely chopped flat leaf parsley

1/2 teaspoon salt
1/4 teaspoon black pepper

1 recipe pilou (see next column)

grated Parmesan cheese

Sauté vermicelli in butter and oil, stirring, until golden. Remove with slotted spoon and reserve.
Add onion and garlic and sauté until soft.
Add tomatoes, stock, parsley and reserved vermicelli. Cover, bring to boil and cook until vermicelli is tender.
Adjust seasonings with salt and pepper and gradually pour over pilou in soup tureen.
Serve with grated Parmesan cheese.
Serves 8 - 10
Or add thinly sliced courgettes, sliced beans, corn, peas or other vegetables at the same time as the vermicelli.

PILOU

3 - 4 egg yolks
3 - 5 tablespoons olive oil

In soup tureen beat egg yolks until fluffy. Gradually add olive oil as if making mayonnaise, beating constantly, until smooth, but not as thick as mayonnaise.

ZUPPA PAVESE

1-1/2 pints any rich stock

4 thick slices French or Italian bread,
  fried in olive oil
4 small eggs

paprika
flat leaf parsley sprigs

Heat stock to boiling.
Place a slice of bread in each of 4 bowls, carefully break an egg onto each, and gradually pour hot soup over the egg to cook it slightly. (Poach the eggs first if you prefer them cooked solid.)
Serve with a sprinkling of paprika and flat leaf parsley sprigs.
Serves 4
Or pass round a bowl of grated Parmesan cheese.

ZUPPA ALLA PISTOU

2 small leeks, white only, thinly sliced
2 stalks celery, sliced thinly on diagonal
2 medium-sized carrots, thinly sliced
2 garlic cloves, finely chopped
2 tablespoons olive oil

2-1/2 pints rich beef, chicken or veal stock
1/2 pound green beans, cut on diagonal

1/2 pound potatoes, peeled and diced
1 bunch spinach, chopped (about 1/2 pound)
1 14-ounce can tomatoes, cut up
1/2 teaspoon thyme
1/4 teaspoon rosemary
1/2 teaspoon black pepper
3/4 teaspoon paprika
1-1/2 teaspoons salt

3 ounces crisp lettuce, shredded
1 recipe pistou (see below)

grated Parmesan cheese

Sauté leeks, celery, carrots and garlic in oil until leeks are soft; do not brown. Add stock, bring to boil and add beans. Cook 5 minutes, add potatoes, spinach, tomatoes and seasonings, and bring back to boil. Cook 10 minutes until potatoes are almost tender. Add lettuce and boil 3 minutes until tender-crisp. Adjust seasonings.

Mix pistou in soup tureen, whisk in 1/4 pint hot soup and gradually beat in rest of soup. Serve with grated Parmesan and extra pistou.

Serves 6 - 8

For heartier meal, add cooked red or white beans, pasta and other vegetables such as courgettes and mushrooms.

PISTOU

1-1/2 teaspoons fresh basil
1 teaspoon finely chopped garlic
1 large tomato, peeled, seeded and diced, or
  1 teaspoon tomato paste
4 tablespoons grated Parmesan or Gruyère cheese

6—8 tablespoons olive oil

Crush basil, garlic and tomato in mortar and transfer to soup tureen. Blend in cheese and gradually add olive oil, beating constantly.

Oriental Soups

An idealist is one who, on noticing that a rose smells better than a cabbage, concludes it will also make better soup.

—H. L. Mencken

Volumes could be written about fascinating Oriental soups never encountered in restaurants. This I discovered under the tutelage of three experts, one Chinese, two Japanese. Especially interesting were the trips to Oriental markets to purchase fuzzy melon, dried fish stomach, seaweed, superior fresh seafoods and myriad other strange or familiar ingredients. Most Americans of European descent are just beginning to appreciate that weird (to them) odors of an Oriental market are far removed from the fragrant broths to be sipped from delicate bowls or centered on the table for individual ladling.

A common misconception is to think of foods of the Orient in terms of mostly Chinese or Japanese. Korea, Indochina, Indonesia, India, Sri-Lanka and other Far East countries have many tasty foods and flavors, too.

For those fortunate enough to live in an area with Oriental neighborhoods, it's easier to build up a supply of dried items for variety in many dishes. They keep indefinitely and need only to be thoroughly washed before using, sometimes soaked to soften.

Dried Chinese mushrooms must *always* be soaked. Cover with lukewarm water for 10 minutes or more, rinse, dry and use as recipe directs. For Japanese recipes, sprinkle with a little sugar when soaking.

The light soy is less salty than the heavier, dark variety and is to be used in all the recipes which follow.

For the more complicated Oriental soups soaking, dicing and other preliminary processing of ingredients should be done well ahead of time. You'll note that some of the soups can be prepared the day before. Refrigerate, and reheat just before serving—a great help to cooks who are also hosts or hostesses.

FISH BALLS

1/2 pound fillets of sole, minced
1 teaspoon cornflour
1/2 teaspoon salt
1/4 teaspoon nutmeg
1 teaspoon melted butter

Mix ingredients, chill and form into small balls.

INDONESIAN FISH BALL SOUP

2-1/2 pints fish stock
2 stalks celery, sliced thinly on diagonal

1 recipe fish balls (see left)

3 ounces bean-thread noodles*, soaked 10 minutes,
  drained and cut into 5-inch lengths
1/2 teaspoon salt
1/4 teaspoon pepper
nutmeg

slivered spring onions
lemon slices

Indonesian cooking has taken ingredients from the Chinese and Japanese; thus the bean-thread noodles.

Combine stock and celery; cover, bring to boil and simmer 10 minutes.
Keep at slow boil and add fish balls; cook 5 minutes or until balls rise to top.
Add bean-thread noodles, salt, pepper and nutmeg. Bring back to boil and cook 2 minutes. Adjust seasonings and serve with slivered spring onions and lemon slices.
Serves 6
Or add peeled, diced winter melon at the same time as the fish balls.

MEAT BALLS

1/4 pound each minced beef and lean pork
1/4 pound mashed potatoes made without butter or
  seasoning (instant is fine)
1/2 teaspoon soy sauce
1/4 teaspoon salt
1/8 teaspoon each mace and nutmeg
1 tablespoon cornflour

Mix ingredients thoroughly, form balls the size of
marbles and chill at least 1 hour. Freeze or use in
soup. Can also be cooked in boiling salted water.

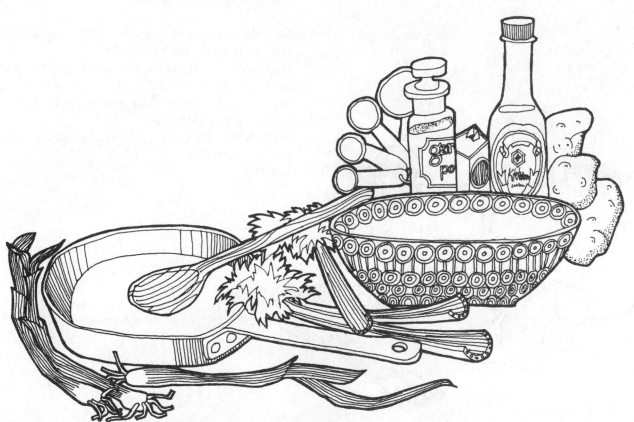

CURRIED TURKEY SOUP

2-1/2 pints rich turkey stock
1 medium-sized onion, chopped
1 tart eating apple, peeled, cored and diced
2 teaspoons curry powder
1/4 teaspoon ground cardamom
1/2 teaspoon salt

3 egg yolks, beaten
1/2 pint buttermilk
1/4 teaspoon garlic powder
6 ounces cooked turkey, cubed

finely chopped parsley
crisp-fried crumbled bacon
almonds sautéed in butter

Simmer stock, onion, apple, curry, cardamom and salt 1/2 hour. Purée in blender.
Beat yolks, buttermilk and garlic powder and add to stock with cooked turkey. Bring just to boil, adjust seasonings to taste and sprinkle with lots of finely chopped parsley.
Serve with crisp-fried crumbled bacon and almonds sautéed in butter.
Serves 6

CURRIED AUBERGINE SOUP

1 tablespoon olive oil
1/4 pound unpeeled aubergine, cubed
4 tablespoons finely chopped spring onions and
  tops
1/2 teaspoon finely chopped garlic
1 tablespoon butter
4 teaspoons flour
1 - 2 teaspoons curry powder
3/4 pint milk
1/4 teaspoon each crushed rosemary and oregano

1/4 pint double cream
salt
pepper

Sauté aubergine in oil until golden. In saucepan,
sauté onion and garlic in butter until onion is soft.
Sprinkle with flour and curry, cook and stir 3
minutes and gradually add milk. Cook and stir until
thickened, add rosemary, oregano and aubergine.
Simmer 15 minutes. Force through sieve, leaving
peel behind.
Heat, add cream and reheat; do not boil. Adjust
seasonings with salt and pepper.
Serves 3

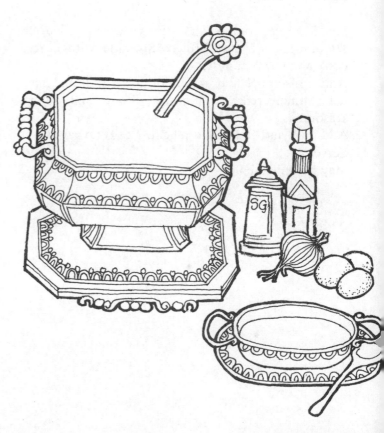

CEYLONESE CONSOMMÉ

1 pound tart eating apples, peeled, cored and diced
1 small onion, finely chopped
2 ounces celery leaves, chopped
3 tablespoons unsalted butter
1 - 2 teaspoons curry powder
3 10-1/2-ounce cans condensed beef consommé
1 soup can water
3/4 pint milk
1/2 pint single cream

Wonderful to serve in the living room before sitting down to dinner.

Sauté apple, onion and celery leaves in butter 10 minutes; do not brown. Sprinkle with curry; cook and stir 3 minutes.
Add consommé and water, bring to boil and simmer, uncovered, 15 minutes. Strain and adjust seasonings.
Add milk and cream and reheat. Needs no garnish.
Serves 6 - 8
May be served cold.

CREAMY CEYLONESE SOUP WITH CURRY PUFFS

1/2 pound tart eating apples, peeled, cored and diced
3 tablespoons grated onion
2 tablespoons butter
1 tablespoon flour
1 - 2 teaspoons curry powder

1-3/4 pints chicken stock
1/4 pint dry white wine

3 egg yolks, beaten
3/4 pint double cream

salt
white pepper
creamy milk

5—6 ounces cooked chicken or prawns, finely chopped

finely chopped chives or spring onion tops

1 recipe curry puffs (see opposite)

Sauté apple and onion in butter 10 minutes without browning. Sprinkle with flour and curry; cook and stir 3 minutes.
Gradually add stock and wine; cook and stir until smooth and slightly thickened. Cover and cook gently 20 minutes. Strain and reheat.
Beat yolks and cream, whisk in 1/4 pint hot soup and return to rest of soup. Cook and stir 3 minutes without boiling. Cool and chill.
Adjust seasonings with salt and pepper, thin with creamy milk if desired, and sprinkle with chicken or prawns. Serve in chilled bowls and garnish with finely chopped chives or spring onion tops. Serve with curry puffs.
Serves 6 - 8
If served hot, garnish with sieved hard-boiled eggs and paprika.

CURRY PUFFS

1 1-pound package phyllo*

1 pound minced beef

3 tablespoons butter

4 tablespoons finely chopped onion

1/8 teaspoon garlic powder

1/2 - 1 teaspoon cumin

1 teaspoon salt

dash cinnamon, ginger powder and cayenne

1/4 pint yoghurt

6—8 tablespoons finely chopped cooked potato

1 hard-boiled egg, chopped

6—8 tablespoons raisins

1 tablespoon lemon juice

Sauté beef until brown, remove from pan and drain. Pour any remaining fat from pan, add butter and sauté onions until soft.

Add seasonings, return meat to pan, cook and stir 3 minutes.

Blend in yoghurt and simmer to absorb almost all the liquid.

Add remaining ingredients, mix well and cool.

When working with phyllo pastry always keep it covered with greaseproof paper and a damp cloth to prevent drying. If the layers break, don't worry, as you can "mend" them with the melted butter as you place layer on layer. Remove 4 layers at a time, spread each with melted butter using a pastry brush, and restack them. Cut into 2-1/2-inch rounds, place 1 teaspoon of filling on rounds and fold over to form a half-moon shape, crimping the edges to seal. Place on a baking sheet and repeat until all the filling is used, making about 30 puffs. Bake in a 350°F/Mark 4/180°C oven 15 minutes or until golden.

Any leftover pastry can be used for strudel, baklava, or even a casing for meat loaf. Seal well and refrigerate up to 5 days.

*Phyllo pastry sheets are available in Greek groceries. I do not recommend frozen phyllo, but if none other is available be sure to let it defrost overnight in the refrigerator before using.

THE ORIENTAL FIREPOT

Strangers become friends and friends get friendlier around an intimate firepot soup. The shiny brass firepot filled with glowing charcoal designed specifically for this soup is spectacular, though not absolutely necessary. Electric casserole cookers or pretty pots or pans over braziers make suitable substitutes.

The seafood, poultry, meat, vegetables and garnishes and seasonings listed are just a few of many you may wish to try. Arrange them attractively on platters and trays where they'll be easily accessible to you and your guests. Surround the pot with individual plates and bowls. The broth should be gently simmering. Everyone picks up his chopsticks and cooks morsels in the broth. Keeping track of whose morsels are whose can be quite a game.

Small individual sieves are best for retrieving the morsels at their parboiled, crunchy best. The retrieved delicacies may be eaten with chopsticks or sandwiched between crisp lettuce leaves. It's advisable to provide Oriental soup spoons, too, for sipping the broth later.

If desired, each guest may break a small egg into his bowl, beat it lightly and dip hot morsels into it before or after seasoning.

When everyone has had his fill of morsels, add bean-thread noodles and 2 beaten eggs to broth; let simmer to set eggs and serve. Or omit beaten eggs and ladle hot soup over eggs left in bowls.

3-3-1/2 pints basic Chinese chicken broth (see page 75)

8 halved scallops
8 prawns, shelled and halved lengthwise
1/4 pound canned abalone, cut in julienne strips
1 fillet of sole, cubed
other firm raw fish in season

1 chicken breast, cut in julienne strips
1/2 pound pork fillet, cut in julienne strips
1/2 pound top sirloin beef, thinly sliced
3 chicken gizzards, scored and thinly sliced

1 bunch small spinach leaves
1 small Chinese cabbage, pulled apart
1 bunch watercress sprigs
4 spring onions, cut in 4-inch pieces
other vegetables in season

4 ounces bean-thread noodles, soaked 10 minutes and cut into 6-inch lengths

In small bowls

hoisin sauce*
mustard
slivered spring onions
toasted sesame seeds

In attractive shake bottles

soy sauce
dry sherry
sesame oil
oyster sauce*
white vinegar

aji oil*

eggs

*see glossary

KOREAN KOOK WITH MANDOO

1/2 pound round steak, cut on diagonal
  into very thin slices
3 spring onions, finely chopped
2 tablespoons soy sauce
1/2 teaspoon finely chopped garlic
1/2 teaspoon peeled and finely chopped fresh ginger
1/2 teaspoon toasted sesame seeds

1-1/2 tablespoons corn oil

1-1/2 pints water
3/4 pint beef stock
1 large dried Chinese mushroom, softened

12 mangetout peas, blanched 2 minutes
1 small square tofu*, diced
1 recipe mandoo (see next column)
slivered spring onions

*see glossary

Marinate meat with spring onions, soy, garlic, ginger
and sesame seeds at least 2 hours.
Heat oil and frizzle meat to brown.
Add water, stock and mushroom. Cover, bring to
boil and simmer 20 minutes. Remove mushroom
and cut into 12 slivers; set aside.
Adjust seasoning with salt.
Arrange 2 mushroom slivers, 2 mangetout peas,
several tofu dice and as many mandoo as desired in
6 bowls. Ladle soup over and sprinkle with slivered
spring onions.
Serves 6

MANDOO

1/2 pound minced lean beef
2 tablespoons Kim Chee*, drained,
  squeezed dry and chopped
4 tablespoons bean sprouts, blanched, drained,
  squeezed dry and chopped
1 tablespoon finely chopped spring onions
1/2 teaspoon very finely chopped fresh ginger

1 teaspoon toasted sesame seeds
1/8 teaspoon each pepper, paprika and sugar
1/2 teaspoon salt
1 teaspoon cornflour
won ton skins (see page 77)

*see glossary

Mix ingredients, fill won ton skins as directed in
won ton soup, and cook in boiling salted water
5 minutes or until they rise to the surface.

ORIENTAL CRAB & CORN BISQUE

3-1/4 pints basic Chinese chicken or
 pork broth (see page 75)
6 fresh mushrooms, sliced, or
6 dried Chinese mushrooms, softened and slivered
1 white onion, sliced
1 can (16-ounce) cream-style corn

sugar
soy sauce
pepper
1/2-3/4 pound flaked crab meat

2 eggs, beaten

fresh coriander sprigs

Simmer stock, mushrooms and onion 30 minutes, adding corn last 10 minutes, keeping at a slow boil. Adjust seasonings with sugar, soy and pepper, add crab and reheat.
Bring to slow boil and gradually drizzle in eggs. Remove from heat and serve immediately. Garnish with fresh coriander sprigs.
Serves 8

THAI SOUP WITH LEMON

1/2 pound fish heads and trimmings
3/4 pound prawns
2 bay leaves
6 peppercorns
1 sliced onion
tops of 4 spring onions, chopped
3 tablespoons lemon juice
1 tablespoon grated lemon rind
2-1/2 pints water

1/2 pound lean pork, cut in julienne strips
1 raw chicken breast, cut in julienne strips

1/2 pound firm white fish fillet,
 cut into 1-inch squares

fish sauce, fish soy*
lemon juice
salt

*see glossary

Shell and devein prawns, dice and reserve. Combine shells, fish heads and trimmings, bay leaves, peppercorns, onion, spring onion tops, lemon juice and rind and water. Cover, bring to boil and simmer 30 minutes; skim off any scum that rises to surface. Strain and reheat. Add pork and cook 10 minutes; add chicken and cook 5 minutes. Bring back to boil, add fish squares and cook gently 5 more minutes. Add diced prawns, bring back to boil and remove from heat.
Season to taste with fish sauce or fish soy, lemon juice and salt.
Serves 6 - 8

Although appearance is important in Chinese cooking, and many of their foods look really spectacular, flavor and texture are even more important.

• When one vegetable or meat is diced, all others in recipe should be diced whenever possible; if slivered, all slivered.

• A dash of sugar often brings out just the flavor you're looking for.

• Soy sauce will darken soup and ingredients, so if you want to keep fish, tofu, chicken and water chestnuts white, let your guests add soy.

• Ingredients can be omitted, increased, or decreased in Chinese soups more than any others. Keep a varied stock on hand for exploring the possibilities.

• Fresh ginger root need not be peeled. Just slice the root, wash and use to flavor.

• There is no substitute for dried tangerine which can be purchased in Chinese markets; sometimes called dried orange peel.

• Rice should be long grain, but not the quick-cooking kind.

Chinese Soups

BASIC CHINESE BROTH

1 pound raw chicken or pork bones
3-1/4 pints water
1 - 2 slices fresh ginger root
dash sugar
salt

This broth is to be used in all Chinese soups.

Combine chicken and/or pork bones with water and ginger; cover, bring to boil, skim off any scum that rises to top, and simmer gently 45 minutes to 1-1/2 hours. Strain and season with sugar and salt.

VARIATIONS: CHINESE BROTH

• Cut Chinese cabbage lengthwise, wash and slice. Add to broth and simmer 10 minutes.

• Add 1 cup diced tofu (see glossary) to broth and simmer 5 minutes.

• Combine the cabbage and tofu in the broth.

• Add dried Chinese mushrooms, softened and slivered, to broth and simmer 20 minutes.

• Cut core end of mustard greens in 1/2-inch slices, cut green part into 2-inch slices; cover with water and wash thoroughly in several changes of water. Drain and add to boiling pork stock that has simmered with an extra slice of ginger root. Bring to boil and cook 5 minutes. Remove ginger and adjust seasonings. (Spinach or Swiss chard can also be used in this way.)

WON TON SOUP

2-1/2 pints basic Chinese chicken or pork broth
  (see page 75)
1 strand dried turnip greens (optional)*,
  washed to remove sand
1 dried tangerine peel*, soaked 10 minutes
4 dried Chinese mushrooms, softened and slivered
salt
soy sauce

24 won tons (see page 77)

fresh coriander sprigs

*see glossary

Simmer broth with turnip greens, tangerine peel and mushrooms for 30 minutes. Remove greens and tangerine peel. Season to taste with salt and soy. Keep hot.
In separate saucepan cook won tons in salted boiling water 4 to 5 minutes until they rise to top; do not boil too hard. Then cook 1 more minute and drain well.
Remove won tons with slotted spoon and place 4 in each of 6 bowls. Fill bowls with hot soup and garnish with fresh coriander sprigs.
Serves 6

WAH WON TON SOUP

2-1/2 pints broth treated as above
3 chicken gizzards, scored and thinly sliced
3 chicken hearts, sliced
6—8 tablespoons slivered (canned) bamboo shoots
3 chicken livers, halved or quartered
3 medium squid, cleaned, halved, and scored lightly
  before slicing bodies and cutting up tentacles
1/4 pound mangetout peas or 1 small bunch bok choy,
  coarsely chopped and well washed
6 large prawns, cleaned and halved lengthwise

24 - 48 won tons (see page 77)

Bring simmered broth to boil, add gizzards and hearts and cook 3 minutes. Add bamboo shoots, livers, squid and vegetable; bring back to boil and cook 2 minutes. Add prawns, bring just to boil and remove from heat. Add won tons, as in won ton soup.
Serves 6 - 8
Or can add pieces of cooked slivered pork and/or chicken, and for a main meal more won tons.

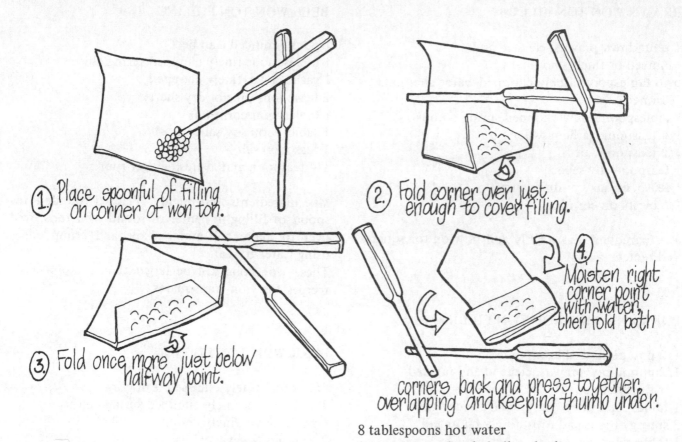

1. Place spoonful of filling on corner of won ton.

2. Fold corner over just enough to cover filling.

3. Fold once more just below halfway point.

4. Moisten right corner point with water, then fold both corners back and press together, overlapping and keeping thumb under.

WON TONS

Ready-made won ton skins are sold in many Chinese and Japanese groceries. If well wrapped, they may be frozen, but the skins dry out more readily and become difficult to manipulate.

Homemade skins are equally as good, but without proper equipment it is difficult to roll them thin enough. The recipe follows in case you can't find them in your area.

8 tablespoons hot water
1 teaspoon each salad oil and salt
about 9 ounces plain flour

Combine hot water, oil and salt; quickly mix in enough flour to make a firm dough. Knead until smooth and pliable.

Roll into 3 or 4 1/2-inch ropes, wrap each in greaseproof paper and refrigerate 30 minutes.

Working with one rope at a time, cut off 1/2-inch slices and roll as thinly as possible into squares or rounds.

Stack, keeping covered, and repeat with remaining ropes.

This recipe makes about 40 skins.

PRAWN WON TON FILLING

1 pound raw prawns, cleaned and
 minced or finely chopped
6—8 tablespoons finely chopped water chestnuts
 (canned)
1 tablespoon finely chopped spring onions
1/4 teaspoon garlic powder
1/2 teaspoon salt
1 teaspoon soy sauce
1 teaspoon sake or dry sherry
1 tablespoon cornflour

Mix ingredients thoroughly and fill won ton squares
as directed.

PORK & PRAWN WON TON FILLING

1/2 pound minced lean pork
1/2 pound raw prawns, cleaned and minced
 or finely chopped
1 tablespoon finely chopped fresh coriander
3 spring onions and tops, finely chopped
1 tablespoon soy sauce
8 water chestnuts (canned), finely chopped
1/2 teaspoon salt
1 tablespoon cornflour
1 egg, beaten

Mix ingredients thoroughly and fill won ton squares
as directed.

BEEF WON TON FILLING

1 pound minced lean beef
1 tablespoons finely chopped spring onions
1 garlic clove, finely chopped
2 teaspoons sake or dry sherry
1 tablespoon cornflour
1 tablespoon soy sauce
1 teaspoon salt
1/4 teaspoon grated fresh ginger root

Mix ingredients thoroughly. Place 1 rounded teaspoon of filling in center of round won tons, fold
over to make half-moon shape and crimp edges,
using water to seal.
These won tons will be larger than the preceding
recipes for won ton squares.

PORK WON TON FILLING

3/4 pound finely chopped lean pork
2 tablespoons finely chopped spring onions
1 garlic clove, finely chopped
2 teaspoons sake or dry sherry
1 tablespoon soy sauce
1 teaspoon salt

Mix ingredients thoroughly and fill won ton squares
as directed.

SEAWEED SOUP

3-1/4 pints Chinese chicken or pork broth
(see page 75)
4 dried Chinese mushrooms, softened and slivered
1 slice fresh ginger root
4 tablespoons dried shrimps*

1 handful of dried, bulk seaweed**, soak in cold
water 10 minutes, washed in three or four
changes of water, and coarsely chopped
1/4 pound minced pork
4 tablespoons diced water chestnuts (canned)

4 tablespoons chopped spring onions

**6 sheets of seaweed may be substituted for the bulk
seaweed, but bulk is tastier and has a better texture
(see glossary).

*see glossary

Combine stock, mushrooms, ginger and shrimps;
cover, bring to boil and simmer 20 minutes.
Add seaweed, pork and water chestnuts; bring to
boil and simmer 15 minutes.
Just before serving, sprinkle with spring onions.
Serves 6 - 8
Can beat in 1 beaten egg at last minute; or add 6
ounces diced tofu (see glossary) or 6 to 8 tablespoons
diced prawns, and bring just to boil.

DICED WINTER MELON SOUP

3-1/4 pints basic Chinese chicken or
  pork broth (see page 75)
2 pounds winter melon, washed, peeled and diced
6 large dried Chinese mushrooms, softened and diced
1 1-inch piece dried tangerine peel*, soaked
  10 minutes
6—8 tablespoons each diced water chestnuts
  and bamboo shoots (canned)
1 raw chicken breast, diced

salt

6—8 tablespoons slivered prosciutto or Westphalian
  ham
fresh coriander sprigs

*see glossary

Combine broth, winter melon, mushrooms, tangerine peel, water chestnuts and bamboo shoots in a large pan; cover, bring to boil, and simmer gently 1 hour, adding diced chicken last 10 minutes.
Discard tangerine peel and adjust seasonings with salt.
Garnish with ham and fresh coriander.
Serves 8 - 10
Or add 8 tablespoons frozen peas, bring just to boil and add 2 tablespoons dry sherry just before serving.

WINTER MELON POND SOUP

Instead of using diced winter melon, the broth, mushrooms, tangerine peel, water chestnuts, bamboo shoots and chicken are cooked in the whole melon and the soup is served from the melon—a spectacular dish!
Buy an evenly shaped melon, about 10 pounds in weight; cut 1/4 off top and set aside. Scrape out the pulp and seeds and set the melon in a bowl that just fits its circumference. Make a string "harness" around bowl and melon, or wrap in double-thick cheesecloth, for easy handling; set on a rack in a large pan. Fill the melon with stock and ingredients, saving any extra stock to serve later. Put top on melon and pour boiling water into pan, filling it 7/8th full. Cover pan and steam gently 3 hours. Lift melon and bowl from pan; remove harness or cheesecloth, discard tangerine peel, and serve, scooping out some of the flesh with each serving.

FUZZY MELON SOUP

1 fuzzy melon (about 1/2 pound)

2-1/2 pints Chinese chicken or pork broth (see page 75)

1 tablespoon dried shrimps*

1 egg, beaten

fresh coriander

*see glossary

A light, before-dinner broth with a delicate flavor that cannot be duplicated.

Scrape fuzz off melon and cut into bite-size slices. Simmer broth and shrimps 20 minutes. Bring broth back to boil, add melon, and cook 5 minutes after broth returns to boil.
Drizzle egg into soup and cook 2 minutes.
Garnish with fresh coriander.
Serves 6

QUICK WATERCRESS SOUP

1-1/2 pints water
1/4 pound minced lean pork
1 slice fresh ginger root
1/2 teaspoon salt
4 tablespoons diced water chestnuts (canned)

2 bunches watercress, large stems removed (about 8 ounces)

6 ounces diced tofu*

*see glossary

Bring water to boil, crumble in pork, and add ginger, salt and water chestnuts. Cook at gentle boil 15 minutes.
Bring to hard boil, add watercress and cook 5 minutes.
Add tofu and cook 3 minutes.
Serves 4 - 6
For easier eating cut up large watercress sprigs.

GOEY GAW

1-1/2 ounces goey gaw*, soaked 1 hour
 in cold water, turning often

4 pints Chinese chicken broth (see page 75)
1 slice fresh ginger root
1 piece dried tangerine peel**
1 raw chicken breast, sliced

1/2 pound mangetout peas

*Blown-up, dried fish maw (stomach). If unobtainable, dried sea slugs (bêche-de-mer), stocked by some Oriental suppliers, may be used instead.
** See glossary

The idea of fish stomach may not appeal to everyone, but the texture is marvelous and the flavor of the soup delicate.

Cut goey gaw down center and then cut into 1-inch dice. Set aside.
Simmer stock, ginger and tangerine peel 20 minutes.
Bring soup to boil, add goey gaw and chicken, bring back to boil and cook 10 minutes.
Add mangetout peas, bring back to boil and immediately remove from heat.
Serves 8

CHINESE OXTAIL – BLACK BEAN SOUP

1 whole lean oxtail, about 1-1/2 pounds,
 cut into 1-1/2-inch lengths, large pieces halved

3-1/4 pints water
1 washed dried tangerine peel*
8 - 10 dried Chinese mushrooms, softened
8 - 10 Chinese red dates, washed, not soaked
1 slice fresh ginger root
3/4 teaspoon salt
1/2 teaspoon sugar

6 ounces black beans, washed and blanched,
 rinsed and then soaked in water to cover
 3 - 4 hours

*see glossary

Blanch oxtails and combine with water, tangerine peel, mushrooms, dates, ginger, salt and sugar.
Cover, bring to boil and simmer 1-1/2 hours.
Add beans and cook 1/2 - 1 hour longer until beans are tender but still hold their shape. Remove tangerine peel and adjust seasonings to taste.
Soup is clear because beans have been blanched.
Serves 8 - 10
Can add 1 teaspoon dry sherry to each bowl when serving.

CHINESE CHICKEN WHISKEY SOUP

1-1/2 pounds chicken wings or other cut
  of choice

2 ounces dried black fungus*, soaked in
  warm water 10 minutes
1/2 cup dried needles*, soaked
  5 minutes in cold water to soften
10 small dried Chinese mushrooms, softened
5 ounces blanched raw peanuts

3 tablespoons corn oil
1/2 teaspoon salt
5 - 8 slices fresh ginger root

1-1/4 pints boiling water
4 tablespoons bourbon whiskey or dry sherry

*see glossary

This is served to Chinese mothers after their babies are born to help them regain their strength. It makes an excellent after-theater soup. Better made the day ahead and reheated. The needles add an unusual sweet flavor.

Remove tips from wings and reserve for future stock. Cut wings at joint and set aside.
Cut out any hard membrane in. fungus and pull apart into bite-size pieces. Set aside. Tie each needle into a knot and set aside.
Heat oil, sprinkle with salt and sauté ginger 2 minutes over high heat. Add wings and brown. Add fungus, mushrooms and peanuts; cook and stir over high heat 1 minute.
Cover with boiling water, add bourbon, cover, bring to boil and simmer 20 minutes, adding needles last 10 minutes of cooking. Just before serving skim off surface fat.
Serves 6

LOTUS ROOT SOUP

3-1/4 pints Chinese chicken or pork broth
  (see page 75)
Chinese red dates, soaked in water to cover until soft
1 strand dried turnip greens (optional)*, well
  washed to remove sand
5 - 6 dried lotus roots*, soaked in water to
  cover 2 hours and halved or quartered, or
1 pound fresh (or canned) lotus root, scraped and
  sliced
1 dried tangerine peel*, soaked 10 minutes
4 - 6 dried Chinese mushrooms, softened
  and slivered

*see glossary

Slice dates, discarding pits; combine with rest of
ingredients and broth; cover saucepan and bring to
boil.
Simmer gently 2 hours.
Remove tangerine peel and turnip green.
Serves 8 - 10

SIZZLING RICE SOUP

1 cup (about 6 ounces) rice, well washed
1-1/2 cups water

2-1/2 pints Chinese chicken broth (see page 75)
1/4 pound button mushrooms, sliced
4 tablespoons sliced water chestnuts (canned)
6 - 8 tablespoons diagonally sliced bamboo shoots
  (canned)
1 raw chicken breast, cut in julienne strips

1/4 pound lettuce or Chinese cabbage, shredded

corn oil

*The sizzle's the secret; don't muff it. Cooking rice
the Chinese way is essential.*

Combine rice and water in a heavy sauté pan and let
stand at least 1 hour. Bring to boil, uncovered, over
high heat, lower heat slightly and boil until water
evaporates.
Cover with a tight lid, reduce heat to its lowest and
cook 1-1/2 hours or until the crust that has formed
can be removed easily from pan.
Refrigerate 1 hour or more and break into bite-size
pieces.
Bring stock to boil, add mushrooms, water chestnuts, bamboo shoots and chicken. Cook 10 minutes, add lettuce or cabbage and bring back to boil.
Cook 1 minute.
While soup is cooking, deep fry rice pieces in corn
oil until golden. Drain on paper towels and keep
hot in a casserole in a 375°F/Mark 5/190°C oven.
The timing is important—both the fried rice and the
soup should be very hot. Bring the casserole to the
table and let your guests watch you pour the soup
over it and enjoy the sizzle. Also the taste!

YUON WINTER SOUP
STICKY RICE FLOUR BALL SOUP

3-1/4 pints Chinese chicken or pork broth (see page 75) cooked with 1 1-inch piece dried tangerine peel* and 1 strand well-washed dried turnip green*

1 1-1/2-pound Chinese turnip**, scraped and cut into julienne strips
10 dried Chinese mushrooms, softened and slivered
3 tablespoons dried shrimps* (optional)
3 -4 Lop Chiang*, sliced on diagonal

1/4 pound lean pork, minced once
dash sesame oil
1 tablespoon each soy sauce and cornflour
1/2 teaspoon salt

2 teaspoons grated fresh orange rind

1 recipe rice flour balls (see next column)

**Chinese turnips are a winter vegetable; use Japanese radishes (daikon) or Chinese cabbage instead if desired, adding the latter for the last 15 minutes of cooking.

*see glossary

To be served as a hearty, cold-weather main meal. Very rich in vitamin B because of the rice flour. The balls have a chewy texture; try more than one before you decide whether or not you like them.

Combine stock, tangerine peel, turnip green, turnip strips, mushrooms and shrimps. Cover, bring to boil and simmer 30 minutes.
Mix pork, sesame oil, soy sauce, cornflour and salt.

Bring soup back to boil, add Lop Chiang slices and pork mixture a teaspoonful at a time; cook 10 minutes.
Discard tangerine peel and dried turnip, taste for salt and just before serving add orange rind.
Place 4 or 5 rice flour balls in each of 8 or 10 bowls, pour soup over and garnish with slivered spring onions.

RICE FLOUR BALLS

1-1/2 cups glutinous Chinese rice flour
1/2 cup hot water

While broth is simmering, make balls or make ahead and store in plastic bag with extra rice flour to prevent sticking.
Measure 1 cup rice flour into bowl and drizzle very hot water over, stirring constantly with chopsticks or fork. Mix thoroughly and then knead until smooth. Roll into 1/2-inch thick ropes, pinch off 1/2-inch pieces and roll into small balls.
Just before soup is ready drop balls into boiling salted water; keep at boil until balls rise to surface and become puffy.

JOOK (CHINESE THICK RICE SOUP-CONGEE)

3-1/4 pints rich turkey broth made from leftover
  cooked turkey carcass
8 dried Chinese mushrooms, softened and slivered
1 large piece dried tangerine peel*
1/2 dried, well-washed turnip green*, sliced
  (optional)

6 ounces raw rice, not washed
1 pint boiling water

3 - 4 sheets dried sheet tofu*, broken into
  bite-size pieces

6 - 12 ounces diced leftover turkey
3 Lop Chiang*, sliced on diagonal

sesame oil
soy
salt

slivered spring onions
fresh coriander sprigs
raw fish slices

*see glossary

Never as a first course—good as a main meal, or for a late supper or breakfast. Bland and interesting. Cold-weather soup. Can be made ahead and reheated over and over again.

Simmer broth, mushrooms, tangerine peel and turnip green while making rice.

Over high heat cook rice in boiling water, stirring occasionally. Keep a kettle of boiling water ready to add as needed. After 15 minutes lower heat slightly. Rice should cook until it is completely broken up and gooey, 30 to 40 minutes.

Add rice to broth, cook and stir occasionally for 1 hour or until broth resembles a gruel. Last 15 minutes add tofu; last 10 minutes add turkey and sausages. Keep adding boiling water as needed. Adjust seasonings with sesame oil, soy and salt. Serve with bowls of slivered spring onions and fresh coriander sprigs, and raw fish slices to dip into hot soup.

Serves 8 - 10

Japanese Soups

Delicacy of flavor, beautiful and artistic garnishes, graceful bowls and ritualistic serving characterize Japanese soups, which are second only to rice in culinary importance. Odd numbers are considered lucky in Japan; even numbers unlucky. Thus the Japanese place odd numbers of each type of morsel in the bowl and odd numbers of people are seated around the table. Bowls are sold in sets of five, not six.

The three major types of soup are:
- *Suimono:* clear, served at the beginning of the meal.
- *Miso:* thickened with crushed and fermented soy beans and served towards the end of a meal or for breakfast.
- *Sumashi-shiru:* main-meal soup like either of the above, only with higher proportions of solids to be served along with rice.
Dashi is the base of all three types. The hot soup often serves to heat the morsels, so whenever possible cover the bowls immediately.

SUIMONO (BASIC DASHI)

Dashi #1
2-1/2 pints water
1 6-inch by 2-inch piece kombu*
3 ounces katsuobushi*
1/8 teaspoon sugar
1/2 teaspoon salt

*see glossary

Break kombu into several pieces, combine with rest of ingredients, bring to boil and cook rapidly 3 minutes. Do not overcook. Strain and reserve kombu and katsuobushi.

Dashi #2
Repeat recipe, using reserved kombu and katsuobushi; boil 5 minutes. This increases the strength of the flavor.

VARIATIONS (DASHI #1 OR #2)

• In salted water parboil 1 prawn per person (cleaned, tail left on) and 3 mangetout peas per person. Place in bowl, add dashi and garnish with tiny lemon peel strip.
• Boil 1 or 3 clams (or 3 mussels) per person in dashi until they open. Garnish with finely chopped chives or spring onion tops.
• Place 1 or 3 small squares raw fillet of sole in each bowl. Pour hot dashi over and garnish with tiny lemon peel strip.
• In salted water, parboil slices of fresh mushroom and somen* (thin noodles); cut somen into 6-inch lengths and tie 5 strands together. Place 3 slices of mushroom and 1 tied somen in each bowl. Pour hot dashi over. Garnish with watercress.
• Place 3 1/2-inch cubes tofu*, 3 cubes precooked or raw vegetable and 1 tiny sliver of cooked chicken in bowl. Pour hot dashi over.
• Place 5 name-take*, drained, in each bowl. Pour hot dashi over and garnish with a tiny carrot curl.
• Soak matsutakefu* in water just to soften. Place 1 in each bowl and pour hot dashi over. Serve immediately.
• Can always add sake—1 tablespoon per 3/4 pint dashi. Pass a bottle of aji oil* for guests who like their's hot.

*see glossary

DASHI WITH LOBSTER

2 pints dashi #
soy sauce

3 small fresh mushrooms, each cut into 5 slices
1 small cucumber, peeled and
 cut into 15 thin slices

6 - 8 ounces cooked lobster, cut into
 25 small cubes

5 small watercress sprigs
5 pieces lemon peel cut into tiny half-moon shapes

Heat dashi, season to taste with soy, bring to boil and add mushroom and cucumber slices. Boil 4 minutes. Do not overcook.
Place 3 mushroom slices, 3 cucumber slices and 5 lobster cubes in each of 5 bowls.
Ladle hot dashi over and garnish with watercress and lemon peel.
Serves 5

DASHI WITH CHICKEN BALLS

2 dried Chinese mushrooms, softened and
   cut into 24 small slivers
1 teaspoon soy sauce
1/2 teaspoon sake or dry sherry
1/4 teaspoon sugar

2-1/2 pints dashi # 1 (see page 88)
salt
soy sauce
1 package age*, cut in halves or thirds (optional)

chicken balls (see below)
lemon peel strips
watercress sprigs

*See glossary

Steam mushroom slivers in soaking water, soy, sake
and sugar 10 minutes.
Bring dashi to boil and adjust seasonings to taste
with salt and soy.
In each of 8 bowls place 3 mushroom slivers, 3
chicken balls and 3 pieces of age. Ladle hot dashi
over and garnish with tiny lemon peel strips and
small watercress sprigs.
Serves 8

CHICKEN BALLS

1/2 pound raw chicken breast, very finely chopped
1 egg white
1 tablespoon cornflour
1 teaspoon salt
2 tablespoons mashed cooked green peas
2 tablespoons blanched bean sprouts,
   squeezed dry and finely chopped
1 teaspoon sake or dry sherry
1 teaspoon soy sauce

Mix ingredients, form into 24 balls, and steam
10 minutes.

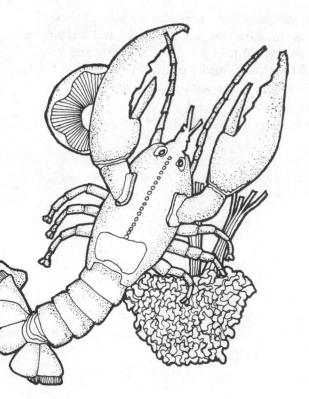

DASHI WITH SHINGIKU (CHRYSANTHEMUM LEAVES)

2 - 3 ounces shingiku*
2-1/2 pints dashi # 2 (see page 88)
salt
soy sauce
2 eggs, beaten

18 tofu* cubes
6 prawns, cleaned, tail left on and cooked
 4 minutes in salted boiling water

raw, fresh mushroom, thinly sliced

*see glossary

Blanch shingiku 3 minutes, drain well and chop.
Cook dashi, salt and soy to taste, and beaten egg over low heat 6 minutes. Add shingiku and reheat. Place 3 tofu cubes and 1 prawn in each bowl. Ladle soup over and serve with a garnish of thinly sliced, raw mushroom.
Serves 6

DASHI WITH UDON

1/2 raw chicken breast, cut into 15 small
 julienne strips
1 teaspoon soy sauce
1/2 teaspoon sake or dry sherry
dash sugar

2 dried Chinese mushrooms, softened and
 cut into 15 slivers
5 water chestnuts (canned), each cut into 5 slices
1/4 pint dashi # 2 (see page 88)
1/4 pound udon noodles*
2-1/2 pints hot water
2 pints dashi # 2
soy sauce

5 tiny raw spinach leaves
5 tiny slivers of raw carrot
5 tiny strips of lemon peel

*see glossary

Marinate chicken strips in soy, sake and sugar 15 minutes. Combine with mushroom slivers, water chestnut slices and dashi. Bring to boil and cook, covered, 10 minutes. Remove cover and let liquid boil away. Set aside and keep warm.
Cover udon with 1-1/2 pints of the hot water, bring to boil and add rest of water. Bring back to boil, cook 1 minute, drain and rinse with cold water. Shake colander to remove as much water as possible.
Heat dashi, adjust seasoning with soy, and reheat with udon.
Place 3 pieces of chicken, 3 mushroom slivers and 5 slices of water chestnuts into each of 5 bowls.
Ladle dashi and udon into bowls and garnish with spinach, carrot and lemon peel.
Serves 5

MISOSHIRU

1-1/4 pints dashi # 2 (see page 88)
5 tablespoons shiromiso or akamiso*

salt
soy sauce
lemon peel
finely chopped chives
aji oil**
*see glossary for miso
**see glossary

Bring dashi to boil, strain miso into dashi and adjust to taste with more miso, salt and soy sauce.
Garnish with lemon peel and finely chopped chives.
Serve with aji oil.
Serves 4

VARIATIONS

• Add 4 ounces tofu**, cut in 1/4-inch dice; cook until tofu rises to surface. Do not overcook.
• Cook diced pumpkin, sliced courgettes, cubed aubergines or potato strips in dashi before adding miso. Garnish with watercress.
• Add bits of bean-thread noodles**, soaked.
• See dashi variations.

**see glossary

MISOSHIRU WITH CHICKEN AND VEGETABLES

scant 3 pints dashi # 2 (see page 88)
4 tablespoons each slivered raw chicken, carrots and mangetout peas
2 tablespoons chopped gobo* or celeriac
6—8 tablespoons diced potatoes

1/4 pint miso*
salt
soy sauce
shichimi pepper* or white pepper

slivered spring onions

*see glossary

Bring dashi to boil, add chicken and vegetables and cook until just tender-crisp.
Add miso, heat and blend; adjust seasonings to taste with salt, soy sauce and shichimi or white pepper.
Garnish with slivered spring onions.
Serves 7

BUTAGIRU

2-1/2 pints Chinese pork broth (see page 75)
2 medium onions, cut in 8ths or 16ths
3/4 pound lean pork, diced
1 tablespoon soy sauce

salt

slivered spring onions or watercress leaves

Japanese pork soup for cold weather; good before a main course of pork chops or cutlets.

Combine first 4 ingredients and cook 1 hour. Adjust seasoning with salt and garnish with slivered spring onions or watercress leaves.
Serves 6

PRAWN BALL SOUP

1-1/4 pints dashi # 1 (see page 88)
3/4 pint water
2 spring onions, cut in 2-inch diagonal lengths
1 teaspoon soy sauce
1 recipe prawn balls (see below)

salt

Combine dashi, water, spring onions and soy; bring to boil and add prawn balls. Cook until balls rise to surface.
Adjust seasonings with salt.
Serves 5

PRAWN BALLS

1 pound uncooked prawns, shelled, cleaned and very finely chopped
1/2 teaspoon grated fresh ginger root
2 tablespoons miso*
2 tablespoons cornflour

*see glossary

Mix ingredients and form into small balls.

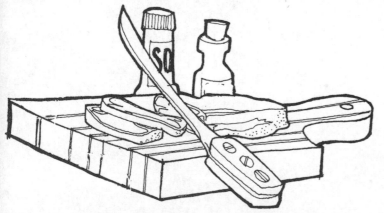

CHAWAN MUSHI

As delicious as it is lovely to look at!

8 medium dried Chinese mushrooms, sprinkled with
  1/2 teaspoon sugar and soaked until
  soft in 1/4 pint water
12 bamboo shoot tips (canned), halved and
  cut into fan shape
8 water chestnuts (canned), cut into 3 slices each

1 tablespoon soy sauce
1/2 teaspoon sugar
1 tablespoon Mirin*

1 large chicken breast
1 teaspoon soy sauce
1/2 teaspoon salt

8 prawns, cleaned, tail left on
1/8 teaspoon salt
2 tablespoons sake or dry sherry

8 gingko nuts (canned)
1 package kamaboko*, sliced, or 4 scallops,
  lightly poached and sliced

4 eggs
2-1/4 cups dashi #1 (see page 88)
1 tablespoon soy sauce
1 teaspoon sugar
1-1/2 teaspoons salt

8 tiny lemon peel strips
8 small watercress sprigs

*see glossary

Cut softened mushrooms into thirds; combine with soaking water, bamboo fans and water chestnuts. Cover, bring to boil and cook 10 minutes. Add soy, sugar and Mirin; cook 5 minutes, remove lid and let liquid boil away.

Cut chicken breast lengthwise and then cut with grain into 40 small strips. Combine with soy and salt.

Sprinkle prawns with salt and coat with sake or dry sherry. Let stand 10 minutes.

Place in 8 chawan bowls: 3 pieces mushroom, 3 bamboo fans, 3 slices water chestnuts, 5 strips chicken, 1 prawn, 1 gingko nut, 1 slice kamaboko.

Beat eggs with chopsticks to blend; do not allow to foam. Add dashi and seasonings and heat slightly. Ladle into bowls, cover, place in steamer and steam 15 minutes; do not allow the water to boil hard at any time. Check; custard should be set and prawns pink.

Garnish with 1 lemon peel strip and 1 watercress sprig; replace lids and serve immediately.

Serves 8

Chawan bowls are traditional Japanese soup bowls with lids, but any heatproof soup bowls (preferably with lids) may be used. If you don't have a steamer, use 2 large saucepans: place 3 heatproof glass bowls on bottom, top with rack and fill with water an inch above the rack. Stand the soup bowls on the rack. Wrap tea towels around the saucepan lids so the condensation drops do not fall into the soup. Everything can be prepared ahead of time—the surprise and delight on the faces of your guests as they view and taste is worth the effort!

From the Americas

Worries go down better with soup than without.
—Yiddish Proverb

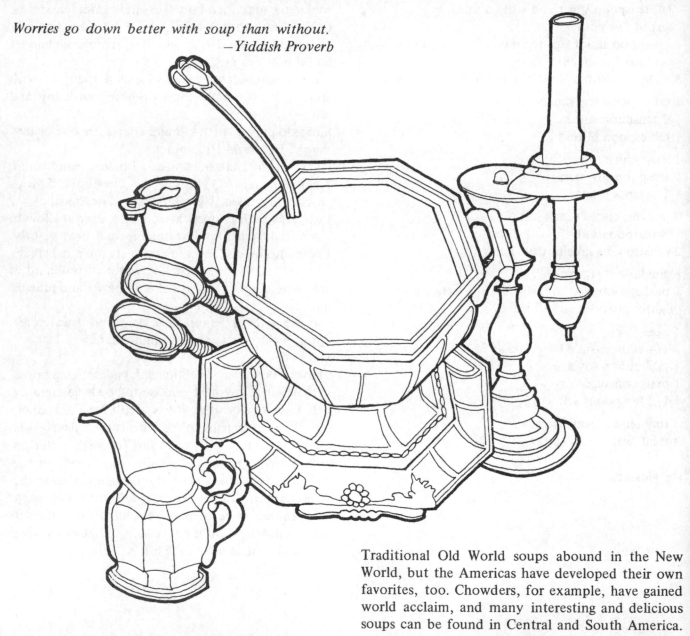

Traditional Old World soups abound in the New World, but the Americas have developed their own favorites, too. Chowders, for example, have gained world acclaim, and many interesting and delicious soups can be found in Central and South America.

ALBÓNDIGAS

1-1/2 pints rich lamb stock
1 large can (28-ounce) peeled tomatoes
4 tablespoons finely chopped green pepper
1 stalk celery and leaves, chopped
2 onions, sliced
6 whole cloves
1 bay leaf
1 tablespoon fresh dill
4 garlic cloves, finely chopped
3 parsley sprigs
12 peppercorns
1/2 tablespoon salt

2 small courgettes, sliced
1/2 pound mushrooms, sliced
1 recipe lamb meat balls (see next column)

dry sherry
sour cream

Bring stock mixture to boil, add courgettes and mushrooms; cook 10 minutes or until courgettes are just tender.
Adjust seasonings, add meat balls, and heat. Serve with 1 tablespoon dry sherry in each bowl and dollops of sour cream.
Serves 6 - 8
Or season with compound chili powder and cinnamon to taste. Or sprinkle with grated Parmesan or sharp Cheddar cheese.

LAMB MEAT BALLS

1-1/2 pounds lean lamb, minced
4 tablespoons freshly grated Parmesan cheese
1 beaten egg
2 tablespoons milk
4 tablespoons finely chopped parsley
1/8 teaspoon rosemary
1 teaspoon black pepper
2 tablespoons lemon juice
4 tablespoons fine burghul (cracked wheat— optional)

Mix ingredients, chill, form into balls the size of large marbles and brown on all sides. If burghul is used, cover and cook 10 minutes.

MEXICAN CHILI SOUP

1-1/2 pints chicken stock
5—6 ounces lean pork, diced
6—8 tablespoons diced onion
6—8 tablespoons fresh corn kernels
1 canned green chili pepper, deseeded and finely
  chopped
1 courgette (about 4 ounces) sliced
1/2 8-ounce can tomato sauce or 6—8 tablespoons
  thick fresh tomato purée

salt
black pepper

avocado balls or cubes
grated Parmesan cheese

Combine ingredients (except avocado and cheese)
and simmer 30 minutes.
Adjust seasonings to taste with salt and pepper. Just
before serving add avocado balls or cubes.
Serve with grated Parmesan cheese.
Serves 4

CHUPE DE CAMARONES

1 medium-sized onion, diced
2 garlic cloves, finely chopped
2 large ripe tomatoes, peeled and diced
1 - 2 teaspoons finely chopped hot chili peppers
1 tablespoon finely chopped fresh oregano or
  marjoram
4 tablespoons olive oil

2-1/2 pints fish stock
1 teaspoon salt
1/2 teaspoon pepper
6 - 8 tablespoons raw rice
3 medium potatoes, halved

1/2 pound fresh or thawed frozen corn kernels
1-1/2 pounds medium-sized prawns, shelled and
  deveined

2 eggs beaten with
4 tablespoons grated cheese

generous 1/4 pint evaporated milk

very finely chopped parsley

Sauté onion, garlic, tomatoes, peppers and oregano
in oil 5 minutes, stirring to blend.
Add stock, salt and pepper; bring to boil, add rice
and potato halves, and cook, covered, 30 minutes,
adding corn last 10 minutes.
Raise heat to boiling, add prawns and cook 5 minutes. Do not overcook.
Drizzle in egg and cheese mixture and boil 1 minute.
Add milk, reheat and adjust seasonings to taste.
Sprinkle with finely chopped parsley and serve
immediately.
Serves 6 - 8

MEXICAN TORTILLA BALL SOUP

1 tablespoon lard
6 tablespoons tomato purée
1/2 teaspoon onion juice
pinch cumin
1/4 teaspoon compound chili powder

3-1/4 pints beef stock
1/2 teaspoon salt
1/4 teaspoon pepper

1 recipe tortilla balls (see next column)

fresh coriander sprigs

Melt lard in a large pan. Add tomato purée, onion juice, cumin and chili powder. Cook and stir 10 minutes over low heat to blend and improve flavors of spices. Combine with stock, season with salt and pepper, cover, bring to boil and simmer gently for 10 to 15 minutes. Adjust seasonings to taste, add tortilla balls and serve with coriander sprigs.
Or add about 1/4 pint each single cream and milk (or 1/2 pint creamy milk), reheat, but do not boil.

BALLS FOR MEXICAN SOUP

1/2 pound white bread, broken up and allowed to
    go stale
1/2 pint milk
4 tablespoons chopped onion
1 garlic clove, chopped
1 egg, beaten
2 tablespoons grated Parmesan cheese
1/4 teaspoon salt, or to taste
ground cumin and cayenne pepper to taste

2 ounces lard, or as needed

Soak bread in milk, distributing evenly. Put through fine blade of mincer with onion and garlic. Combine with egg, cheese and seasonings. Form into 1-inch balls and sauté slowly in lard, on all sides until golden, making sure they do not stick together.
Makes approximately 40 balls

CHUPE HAMBURGO

2 medium-sized onions, finely chopped
4 - 8 tablespoons very finely chopped green pepper
1 garlic clove, finely chopped
2 tablespoons butter and/or oil

1-1/2 pounds minced beef
1/2 pound mushrooms, finely chopped
4 large carrots, grated
2 10-1/2-ounce cans condensed cream of
  mushroom soup
2-1/4 pints canned vegetable or tomato juice,
  or combination
1/2 - 1 teaspoon basil
1 teaspoon salt
1/2 teaspoon paprika
1/4 teaspoon cumin
1/4 teaspoon pepper
1 1-pound can red kidney beans, drained

grated Parmesan cheese
cheese squares (see page 182)

Sauté onions, green pepper and garlic in butter and/or oil until vegetables are soft.
Raise heat, add meat and mushrooms and cook and stir with fork until meat loses its color. Add remaining ingredients (except cheeses), mix well, bring to boil, cover, and simmer gently 1/2 hour. Adjust seasonings to taste. Sprinkle with freshly grated Parmesan cheese and serve with cheese squares.
Serves 6 - 8
Or instead of tomato juice, use beef stock and fresh tomatoes, peeled, seeded and chopped. Add chunks of processed cream cheese and heat until partially melted.

AVOCADO GAZPACHO

1/2 pint sour cream
1/4 pint milk
1/2 pint each tomato juice and tomato sauce
2 tablespoons lemon juice
1 tablespoon olive oil
1 garlic clove, very finely chopped
1 bay leaf
1 cucumber, peeled, seeded and finely chopped
1 tomato, peeled, seeded and diced
salt
black pepper
Tabasco

2 avocados, peeled and stoned
1 tablespoon lemon juice

very finely chopped cucumber, tomato and green
   pepper, garlic fingers (see page 181)

Beat sour cream well, then beat in milk, tomato
juice, tomato sauce, lemon juice, oil and garlic.
Combine well, add bay leaf, cucumber and tomato.
Season with salt, pepper and Tabasco and chill
thoroughly to blend flavors.
Remove bay leaf. Mash the avocados with lemon
juice and blend into tomato mixture just before
serving. Adjust seasonings and serve in chilled
bowls. Garnish with finely chopped cucumber,
tomato and green pepper, and serve with garlic
fingers.
Serves 3 - 4

SPICY GUACAMOLE WITH PRAWNS

1 large avocado, peeled and diced
1/2 pint buttermilk
1/4 pint yoghurt
1 tablespoon mayonnaise
1 tablespoon finely chopped spring onions
2-1/2 tablespoons lemon juice
1 large tomato, peeled and diced
1 - 2 canned green chilis, deseeded and finely chopped
1/8 teaspoon each cumin and coriander

fresh or canned prawns
fresh coriander

Purée ingredients (except prawns and coriander) in
blender and chill. Adjust seasonings and serve in
chilled bowls; garnish with chilled fresh or canned
prawns and fresh coriander.
Serves 3 - 4

SWEET POTATO SOUP

1 medium-sized onion, chopped
3 stalks celery, chopped
1 pound sweet potatoes, peeled and sliced
1 tablespoon bacon fat
2 pints chicken stock
1/2 teaspoon salt
1/4 teaspoon black pepper
nutmeg

sour cream

Sauté onion, celery and sweet potatoes in bacon fat 5 minutes. Add stock, cover, bring to boil and simmer until soft.
Purée in blender and reheat. Season to taste with salt, pepper and nutmeg. Serve with a bowl of sour cream.
Serves 6

VEGETABLE GUMBO

4 tablespoons finely chopped onion
4 tablespoons finely chopped celery
2 tablespoons finely chopped green pepper
2 tablespoons bacon fat

1 teaspoon freshly grated lemon peel
1 bay leaf
3 tablespoons finely chopped parsley
3 large tomatoes, peeled and diced, or
  1 can (14-ounce) tomatoes, broken up
1 garlic clove, finely chopped
1/2 teaspoon black pepper
1/2 teaspoon salt
1/4 teaspoon cumin
2-1/2 pints chicken stock
1/2 pound fresh corn kernels
1/2 pound fresh okra, sliced

leftover chicken bits
leftover ham bits
sausages, sliced and cooked

1/2 teaspoon filé powder*

crisp-fried crumbled bacon

*see glossary

Brown onion, celery and green pepper in bacon fat. Combine with lemon peel, bay leaf, parsley, tomatoes, garlic, seasonings and stock. Cover, bring to boil and cook 10 minutes.
Add corn and okra and cook over high heat 8 minutes, stirring occasionally. Add chicken, ham and sausage.
Remove bay leaf, reheat and adjust seasonings to taste. Add filé powder just before serving. Sprinkle with crisp-fired crumbled bacon.
Serves 6 - 8

CREAM OF SCALLOP SOUP

1 pound scallops, cut in 1/2-inch pieces
juice of 1 or 2 limes
3/4 pint canned clam juice or
  3/4 pint mixed chicken stock and fish stock
1 tablespoon butter
4 tablespoons chopped green pepper (optional)
2 spring onions and tops, sliced
1/4 teaspoon each Worcestershire sauce, garlic
  powder and dry mustard

2 egg yolks, beaten
1/4 pint single cream
1/4 pint milk

paprika
finely chopped parsley, chives and spring onions

Marinate scallops in lime juice several hours. Drain and dry with paper towels.
Sauté green pepper and spring onions in butter 3 minutes, add clam juice and seasonings, bring to boil, add scallops and simmer 4 to 5 minutes until scallops are just done. Be careful—overcooking toughens them.
Beat yolks with cream, add milk and 1/4 pint hot soup and return to rest of soup. Reheat but do not boil.
Adjust seasonings to taste, sprinkle with lots of paprika and finely chopped parsley, chives and spring onions. Serve with pumpernickel toast.
Serves 3 - 4

GARLIC SOUP

20 - 25 garlic cloves, peeled
4 tablespoons olive oil

3-1/4 pints chicken stock
1 chicken stock cube
1 teaspoon soy sauce
1/4 teaspoon each sage and black pepper
2 whole cloves
1/2 teaspoon each oregano, thyme and paprika
8 parsley sprigs

6 - 8 tablespoons dry sherry

8 toasted French bread slices
8 tablespoons each grated Gruyère and Parmesan
  cheese

Sauté garlic in oil until just starting to turn golden. Add stock, stock cube, seasonings and herbs. Cover, bring to boil and simmer 1 hour.
Strain, reheat and adjust seasonings. Just before serving add sherry.
Ladle soup into heated ovenproof bowls, top with toast, sprinkle with 1 tablespoon of each cheese, and grill until cheese has melted.
Serves 8
Or omit cheese. Top each piece of toast with a small raw egg. Ladle hot soup over to poach egg and garnish with coriander.

CREAMY LOBSTER SOUP WITH CHEESE

1 8-ounce lobster tail, cooked and finely chopped
4 tablespoons dry sherry

3 tablespoons onion very finely chopped
1 teaspoon very finely chopped shallot
2 tablespoons celery very finely chopped
2 tablespoons butter

1-1/2 tablespoons flour
1/4 pint double cream
1/2 pint milk

2 tablespoons very finely chopped parsley

1/2 teaspoon salt
1/4 teaspoon garlic powder
1/4 teaspoon white pepper
lemon juice

4 tablespoons grated Provolone cheese
milk
paprika
finely chopped Chinese chives*

*see glossary

Soak lobster in sherry at least 1 hour.

Steam onion, shallots, and celery in butter, covered, 10 minutes.

Sprinkle with flour, cook and stir 3 minutes and gradually add cream and milk. Cook and stir until smooth and slightly thickened.

Add lobster and sherry, and parsley. Reheat and season with salt, garlic powder, pepper and lemon juice to taste.

Just before serving add cheese and heat to melt. Thin with milk if desired.

Dust with paprika and sprinkle with finely chopped Chinese chives.

Serves 3 - 4

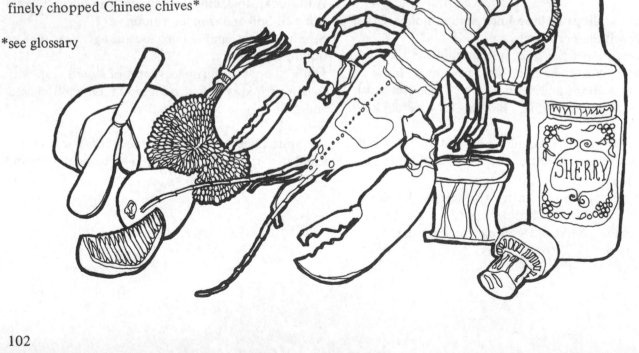

CREAMY CLAM SOUP WITH SPINACH

3 tablespoons finely chopped onion
2 tablespoons butter
1 tablespoon finely chopped shallots
1 garlic clove, finely chopped

1-1/4 pounds frozen chopped spinach, thawed
1/4 teaspoon black pepper
1/2 teaspoon fish seasoning

2 7-1/2-ounce cans minced clams and juice

1 - 2 tablespoons lemon juice
1/2 pint milk
1/4 pint double cream

grated Parmesan cheese

Sauté onions in butter until soft. Add shallots and garlic, and cook 3 minutes. Add spinach, pepper and fish seasoning; cover and cook until spinach is tender.
Purée half of spinach mixture in blender with 1 can clams. Remove to saucepan and repeat with remaining clams and spinach.
Combine spinach and clams with lemon juice, milk and cream; reheat but do not boil. Adjust seasonings to taste and serve with a sprinkling of freshly grated Parmesan cheese.
Serves 4
Or season with nutmeg. Serve very cold in chilled bowls, garnished with hard-boiled egg slices, lemon slices and finely chopped parsley.

CREAM OF CLAM BROTH

1 pint canned clam juice
scant 1/2 pint water
1 chicken stock cube
1/2 pint milk
6 tablespoons double cream

3 tablespoons finely chopped shallots
2 tablespoons butter
2 tablespoons flour

Tabasco
white pepper
salt

5 - 6 tablespoons dry white wine
finely diced butter

paprika
very finely chopped spring onion tops

Combine clam juice, water, stock cube, cream and milk; heat without boiling.
Sauté shallots in butter until soft, sprinkle with flour and stir and cook 3 minutes. Gradually add clam mixture; stir and cook until smooth and slightly thickened.
Season with Tabasco, pepper and salt, and adjust to taste.
Just before serving add wine, swirl in diced butter and sprinkle with paprika and very finely chopped spring onion tops.
Serves 6
Or ladle into ovenproof bowls, top with whipped cream and brown under the grill. Sprinkle with finely chopped chives.

CRAB SOUP WITH PASTA

1 pound flaked crabmeat
4 tablespoons dry sherry

2 stalks celery, finely chopped
1 small onion, finely chopped
6 - 8 tablespoons green pepper finely chopped
3 tablespoons butter

1 teaspoon flour
1/2 teaspoon sugar
1 teaspoon compound chili powder

1/4 pint single cream
1/2 pint milk

4 tablespoons small shell pasta, cooked *al dente* in
  salted boiling water

1/2 teaspoon salt
1/4 teaspoon white pepper
1/2 teaspoon Worcestershire sauce

whipped cream
finely chopped parsley

Very rich—quite thick!

Combine crab and sherry and marinate at least 1 hour.
Sauté celery, onion, and green pepper in butter until vegetables are tender.
Sprinkle with flour, sugar and chili; cook and stir 3 minutes.
Gradually add cream and milk; cook and stir until smooth and slightly thickened.
Add crab, sherry and pasta. Reheat without boiling and season with salt, pepper and Worcestershire sauce. Adjust to taste.
Garnish with whipped cream dollops and finely chopped parsley. Pass round the peppermill.
Serves 4

BONGO-BONGO

4 tablespoons finely chopped mushrooms
1 tablespoon butter
1/2 tablespoon flour
3/4 pint milk
8 ounces fresh oysters and liquid
3 ounces chopped frozen spinach, cooked
  and well drained

1/4 teaspoon garlic powder
1 teaspoon Worcestershire sauce
1/2 teaspoon each thyme, salt and black pepper
1/4 pint double cream

lemon slices

Sauté mushrooms in butter until soft, sprinkle with flour and cook and stir 3 minutes. Gradually add milk; cook and stir until smooth and slightly thickened. Purée in blender with oysters and spinach. Reheat with seasonings and cream; adjust to taste. Cool, chill and serve in chilled bowls with lemon slices.
Serves 4 - 6
To serve hot, heat with 2 tablespoons butter and garnish with double cream whipped with soy sauce.

POACHED FISH IN BROTH

2-1/2 pints basic fish stock (see page 16) fortified
 with white wine, tarragon and lemon juice

3 haddock fillets (or other firm fish)
aioli sauce (see page 179) or
 anchovy-egg sauce (see next column)

lemon wedges
finely chopped parsley

Bring stock to boil and adjust seasonings to taste.
Lower heat and gently poach fish 10 minutes or
until tender. Do not overcook.
Place half a fillet in each soup bowl; top with a
tablespoon of sauce and a portion of stock.
Garnish with lemon wedges and sprinkle with parsley.
Serves 6
Or cut down on proportions and serve as a soup
appetizer.
If thicker soup is desired, bind with a liaison of 2
egg yolks beaten into 1/4 pint hot soup and
returned to rest of soup.

ANCHOVY-EGG SAUCE

3 hard-boiled eggs, sieved
1-1/2 teaspoons cream
1 - 1-1/2 teaspoons anchovy paste
2 drops Tabasco
1/2 - 3/4 teaspoon Worcestershire sauce
3 - 4 tablespoons mayonnaise

Mix ingredients and adjust seasonings to taste.

COLD PRAWN BISQUE

1-1/2 pounds raw prawns, cleaned and deveined
lemon juice

3/4 pint milk
1/2 pint single cream
4 tablespoons each finely chopped onion
  and celery
1/2 - 1 teaspoon anchovy paste
bouquet garni of:
  1 sprig thyme
  3 sprigs parsley
  6 peppercorns
  1 small bay leaf
1-1/2 tablespoons raw rice

scant 1/2 pint double cream

Tabasco
salt
white pepper
Worcestershire sauce

pimiento strips

Cook 1/2 pound of the prawns in rapidly boiling salted water with lots of lemon juice 4 to 5 minutes until pink; do not overcook. Dice and reserve.

Combine rest of prawns, milk, single cream, onion, celery, anchovy paste, bouquet garni and rice. Cover, bring to gentle boil, and simmer 45 minutes, stirring occasionally.

Discard bouquet garni, and purée bisque in blender. Add double cream and chill. Adjust seasonings with Tabasco, salt, pepper and Worcestershire sauce, and serve in chilled bowls. Garnish with reserved prawns and pimiento strips.

Serves 4 - 6

Or sprinkle with finely chopped fresh dill.

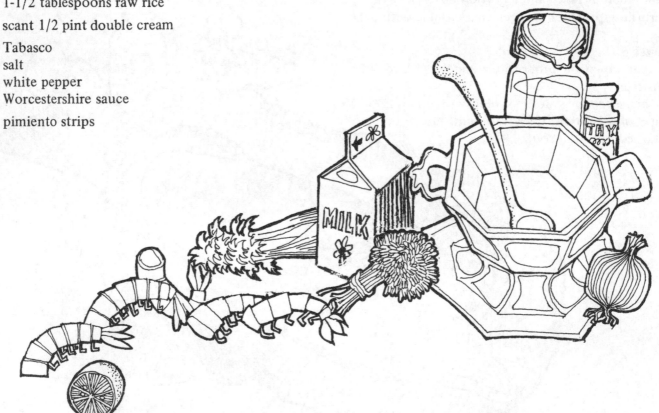

HOT PRAWN BISQUE

2 pounds raw prawns, cleaned and deveined

3 tablespoons butter
2 tablespoons each finely chopped carrot, onion
  and celery
1 garlic clove, finely chopped

1 bay leaf
1/2 teaspoon thyme
3 tablespoons finely chopped parsley
1 tablespoon lemon juice
3/4 pint chicken stock
scant 1/2 pint fish stock

scant 1/2 pint creamy milk
1/4 pint double cream
salt
white pepper
Tabasco
Worcestershire sauce
6 - 8 tablespoons dry white wine

finely chopped fresh dill

Finely chop 1-1/2 pounds of the prawns and set aside. Melt butter until bubbly and over high heat sauté the rest of the prawns with carrot, onion, celery and garlic 5 to 8 minutes, stirring constantly. Do not overcook. Remove prawns, dice and reserve. Combine chopped raw prawns, bay leaf, thyme, parsley, lemon juice and stocks. Cover, bring to boil and simmer 45 minutes, stirring occasionally.
Discard bay leaf. Purée mixture in blender and reheat with milk, cream and reserved prawns. Adjust seasonings to taste with salt, pepper, Tabasco and Worcestershire sauce.
Just before serving add wine. Serve with a generous sprinkling of finely chopped dill.
Serves 4 - 6

COLD BUTTERMILK-PRAWN BISQUE

1-1/2 pounds raw prawns, cleaned and deveined
1-1/4 pints water
1 tablespoon salt
4 tablespoons lemon juice

1-1/4 pints buttermilk
1 cucumber, peeled, seeded and grated
2 tablespoons Dijon-style mustard
1/2 teaspoon prepared horseradish
1/4 teaspoon each sugar and garlic powder
1/2 teaspoon salt
1/2 teaspoon dried dill
1 tablespoon very finely chopped celery
lemon juice

2 tablespoons finely chopped chives

finely chopped parsley

Bring water, salt and lemon juice to rolling boil, add prawns and boil 4 to 5 minutes until pink. Do not overcook. Drain and plunge into ice water. Cut 1/2 cup of prawns into 1/2-inch dice and reserve.
Coarsely chop remainder and purée in blender with 1/2 pint of the buttermilk.
Combine with rest of buttermilk, cucumber, seasonings, celery and a squeeze of lemon juice.
Chill and adjust seasonings to taste.
Stir in chives, serve in chilled bowls and top with reserved diced prawns and finely chopped parsley.
Serves 6

MUSSEL & LEEK BISQUE

4 small leeks, white and some green, finely chopped
4 tablespoons each finely chopped celery and onion
2 cloves garlic, finely chopped
3 tablespoons finely chopped carrot
4 tablespoons butter and/or rendered chicken fat

1-1/2 pints rich beef stock
1/2 pound potatoes, peeled and diced

3 pounds mussels, steamed open and coarsely chopped (discard any that remain closed after steaming)

1/4 pint single cream
1/4 pint milk

salt
white pepper
black pepper
celery salt
lemon juice
1 ounce butter, finely diced

very finely chopped parsley and garlic
paprika

Sauté leeks, celery, onion, garlic and carrot in butter and/or fat until leeks are soft.
Add stock and potatoes, cover, bring to a boil and simmer until potatoes are soft. Purée in blender. Combine potato mixture with mussels and their liquor; add cream. Reheat, but do not boil. Season to taste with salt, white and black pepper, celery salt and a squeeze of lemon juice. Stir in diced butter.
Sprinkle with lots of very finely chopped parsley and garlic, and paprika.
Serves 6 - 8
For richer bisque, add double cream.

ABALONE CHOWDER

3 ounces finely chopped spring onions, leeks and/
  or onions
1 garlic clove, finely chopped
1/4 pound diced salt pork
3 tablespoons butter
3/4 pint chicken stock
scant 1/2 pint fish stock or clam juice
1/2 pound floury potatoes, peeled and diced
1/4 teaspoon celery salt
1/4 teaspoon black pepper

1 1-pound can abalone, drained and finely chopped*
1/4 pint double cream
1/2 pint milk
1/2 teaspoon anchovy paste

salt

lemon juice
1 ounce butter, finely diced
paprika

*If canned abalone are not available, use poached
scallops instead.

Sauté onions, garlic and salt pork in butter until
onions are soft.
Add stocks, potatoes and seasonings; cover, bring to
boil and simmer 10 minutes. Potatoes should stay
firm.
Add abalone, cream, milk and anchovy paste. Blend
well and reheat without boiling.
Adjust seasonings with salt and a squeeze of lemon
juice; swirl in diced butter and sprinkle with paprika.
Serves 6

CRAB CHOWDER

4 slices bacon, diced
2 tablespoons flour
1-1/4 pints milk, or half milk and half single cream
1 tablespoon onion juice
scant 1/2 pint tomato juice
1/4 teaspoon each basil, marjoram, garlic powder
  and black pepper

6 ounces cooked diced potatoes
1 pound flaked crab meat

salt
or celery salt

paprika
reserved bacon bits

Sauté bacon until crisp, remove with slotted spoon
and reserve. Pour off all but 1-1/2 tablespoons of
fat.
Sprinkle with flour and cook and stir 3 minutes.
Gradually add milk and/or cream; cook and stir
until smooth and slightly thickened.
Add onion juice, tomato juice and seasonings; sim-
mer, covered, 10 minutes.
Add potatoes and crab, reheat and adjust seasonings
to taste with salt or celery salt.
Sprinkle with paprika and reserved bacon bits.
Serves 4

TROUT CHOWDER

5 large trout
3/4 pint water
bouquet garni of
  2 parsley sprigs
  1 bay leaf
  6 - 8 tablespoons celery leaves
  1 sprig thyme
  1/2 medium onion stuck with
  2 cloves

6 - 8 tablespoons diced onions
6 - 8 tablespoons diced celery
4 tablespoons diced carrot
3 tablespoons butter
1/2 pound potatoes, peeled and diced
3/4 pint milk
1/4 pint double cream

salt
white or black pepper
garlic powder
celery seed

Cook trout in water with bouquet garni until it flakes when tested with a fork. Remove and set aside to cool. Discard bouquet garni, add vegetables, cover, bring to boil and simmer 5 minutes. Add butter and potatoes and cook until potatoes are just soft.
Add milk and reheat. While vegetables are cooking, remove meat from trout to make about 1-1/4 pounds.
Add to hot chowder with double cream; reheat but do not boil.
Season and adjust to taste. Serve with French bread and unsalted butter.
Serves 6 - 8

110

CLAM CHOWDER

3 - 4 ounces spring onions, leeks and/or onion,
  finely chopped
1 garlic clove, finely chopped
1/4 pound diced salt pork
3 tablespoons butter

1-1/4 pints rich chicken stock
3/4 pound floury potatoes, peeled and diced
1 bay leaf
1/4 teaspoon thyme
1/8 teaspoon allspice
1/4 teaspoon black pepper
3 7-1/2-ounce cans minced clams

1/2 pint double cream
1/2 pint milk

salt
finely diced butter

paprika
slivered spring onions

Sauté onions, garlic and salt pork in butter until onions are soft.
Add stock, potatoes, bay leaf, thyme, allspice and pepper. Cover, bring to boil and simmer 10 minutes. Potatoes should remain firm. Remove bay leaf.
Add minced clams to soup with juices, cream and milk, and reheat without boiling.
Season with salt and adjust to taste.
Stir in diced butter and sprinkle with paprika and slivered spring onions.
Serves 6
For garlic lovers, finely chopped raw garlic sprinkled on top of soup just before serving adds a real zest.

CORN CHOWDER

fresh raw corn kernels from
 4 - 5 large fresh ears of corn*
1-1/4 pints chicken stock
1/2 teaspoon sugar
1/2 teaspoon salt
6—8 tablespoons finely chopped onion
4 tablespoons finely chopped celery
2 ounces butter
1/2 teaspoon dry mustard
1/2 teaspoon sugar
1/4 teaspoon black pepper
1 tablespoon lemon juice
1/2 pound potatoes, peeled and diced, (optional)

1/2 pint single cream
scant 1/2 pint milk

3 drops Tabasco
1/2 teaspoon Worcestershire sauce

1 egg yolk, beaten
1/4 pint double cream

3/4 teaspoon salt
1/4 teaspoon thyme

paprika
finely chopped parsley

*Defrosted frozen corn (8-10 ounces) may be used,
but the flavor is not the same.

Cut kernels from corn, scraping as much pulp and milk off as possible. Boil cobs in stock with sugar and salt 15 minutes. Strain and reserve stock.

Sauté kernels, onion and celery in butter with mustard, sugar and pepper until onions are soft but not browned.

Add lemon juice, reserved stock and potatoes, if used. Cover, bring to boil and simmer 15 minutes. Add cream, milk, Tabasco and Worcestershire sauce. Reheat. Beat yolk and double cream, whisk in 1/4 pint hot soup and return to rest of soup. Heat but do not boil.

Season with salt and thyme and adjust to taste.

Serve sprinkled with paprika and finely chopped parsley.

Watercress and hot French-fried onions also make a good garnish.

111

Other Ports of Call

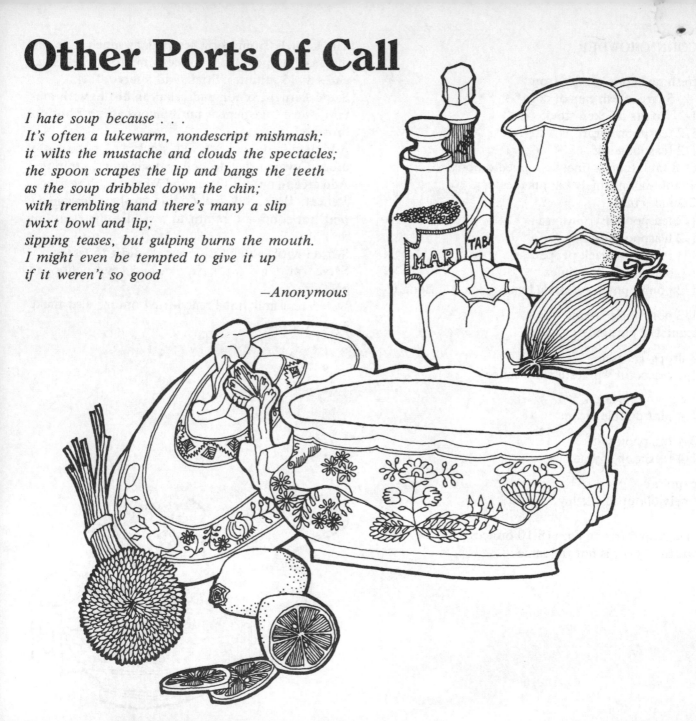

I hate soup because . . .
It's often a lukewarm, nondescript mishmash;
it wilts the mustache and clouds the spectacles;
the spoon scrapes the lip and bangs the teeth
as the soup dribbles down the chin;
with trembling hand there's many a slip
twixt bowl and lip;
sipping teases, but gulping burns the mouth.
I might even be tempted to give it up
if it weren't so good

—*Anonymous*

CHEESE AND ONION SOUP

1 large onion, finely chopped
2 ounces butter
3 tablespoons flour
1/2 teaspoon seasoned salt
1/8 teaspoon cayenne pepper
1/4 teaspoon black pepper
1/2 teaspoon paprika
1/4 teaspoon sage
1-1/2 pints milk
1/4 pint double cream
6 ounces sharp Cheddar cheese, grated
1/2 teaspoon Worcestershire sauce
3 drops Tabasco
3 tablespoons finely chopped parsley

whipped cream
finely chopped chives

This is a very rich soup!

Sauté onion in butter until soft. Add flour and seasonings, cook and stir 3 minutes and gradually add milk and cream. Cook and stir until smooth and thickened. Add cheese and stir until melted. Stir in Worcestershire sauce, Tabasco and parsley, and adjust seasonings to taste.
Garnish with dollops of whipped cream and sprinkle with finely chopped chives.
Serves 6
Or for milder flavor, substitute a milder Cheddar cheese.

CREAMY GREEN PEPPER SOUP

2 small green peppers, diced
6 - 8 tablespoons diced onion
1 garlic clove, finely chopped
2 tablespoons butter

2 tablespoons flour
1/2 teaspoon marjoram
1-1/4 pints chicken stock

3/4 pint milk and/or single cream

1/4 teaspoon white pepper
1/8 teaspoon grated lemon rind

salt

raw green pepper, sliced paper thin
lemon slices

Sauté green pepper, onion and garlic in butter until soft.
Sprinkle with flour and marjoram; cook and stir 3 minutes. Gradually add stock, cook and stir until smooth and slightly thickened, cover and simmer gently 30 minutes.
Purée in blender, add milk and/or cream and season with pepper and lemon rind. Reheat and adjust seasonings with salt; or chill and adjust seasonings.
Garnish with green pepper slices and/or lemon slices.
Serves 4 - 6

BLACK OLIVE SOUP

8 ounces pitted ripe olives, sliced
3 tablespoons grated onion
2 garlic cloves
generous 1-1/2 pints rich chicken stock

2 eggs, beaten
1/4 pint single cream
1/4 pint milk
1 teaspoon Worcestershire sauce
1/2 teaspoon celery salt

salt — be careful!
Tabasco
lemon juice

paprika
grated onion

*see glossary

Simmer olives, onion and garlic in stock, covered, for 20 minutes. Discard garlic.
Beat eggs into cream, beat in 1/4 pint hot stock, and return to rest of soup, together with milk. Season with Worcestershire sauce, celery salt and a squeeze of lemon juice. Adjust to taste with salt and Tabasco, reheat and serve with a sprinkling of paprika and more grated onion.
Serves 4
Or cool, chill and serve in chilled bowls with a sprinkling of finely chopped parsley.

DANISH PORT SALUT SOUP

6 ounces kohlrabi or young turnips,
  peeled and diced
4 tablespoons each finely chopped onion and
  white part of leeks
2 tablespoons butter
12 ounces potatoes, peeled and diced
1-1/4 pints chicken stock
3/4 pint milk
1 can (1-pound) red kidney beans

scant 1/2 pint double cream
6 - 8 ounces Port Salut cheese, grated
salt
white pepper

1 ounce butter, finely diced
finely chopped spring onions
finely chopped parsley

Sauté kohlrabi or turnips, onions and leeks in butter until soft but not browned. Add potatoes, stock, milk and beans; cover, bring to boil and simmer gently 45 minutes. (Will look curdled, but it doesn't matter.)
Add cream and three-quarters of the cheese; cook and stir to melt cheese and reheat; do not boil. Season to taste with salt and white pepper, stir in diced butter and serve with spring onions, parsley and remaining cheese on top.
Serves 6 - 8

BONE MARROW SOUP WITH VEGETABLES

3 pounds beef marrow bones, sawed into
  3-inch pieces*
1 large onion, chopped
4 garlic cloves, finely chopped
2-1/2 pints water
1 teaspoon salt
1/2 teaspoon black pepper

1 large carrot, thinly sliced
1 small onion, thinly sliced
2 stalks celery, sliced thinly on diagonal

3 large tomatoes, peeled and diced

6 - 7 ounces barley, cooked 1-1/2 hours in
  salted water and drained

beef stock

finely chopped fresh herbs

*If you want to keep the marrow intact, wrap each
bone in cheesecloth and tie securely.

*This soup has an unusual, delicate flavor. The recipe
seems complicated only because of the necessity to
remove the fat from the marrow gradually.*

Combine bones, onion, garlic, water, salt and pepper. Cover, bring to boil and simmer 1-1/2 hours.
Skim off any scum that rises to surface.
Cool, chill and defat. Reheat and continue cooking
1-1/2 hours, skimming surface as needed.
Cool, chill and defat. Remove bones and marrow.
Cut up as much marrow as desired and reserve.
Strain soup, bring to boil and add carrot, onion
and celery. Cook 10 minutes and add tomatoes.
Cook 2 more minutes, add barley and reserved
marrow and heat. Adjust seasonings to taste and
add stock if barley has made the soup too thick.
Sprinkle with finely chopped fresh herbs and serve
with strips of cheese.
Serves 6
Or can season with mace and powdered cloves to
taste.

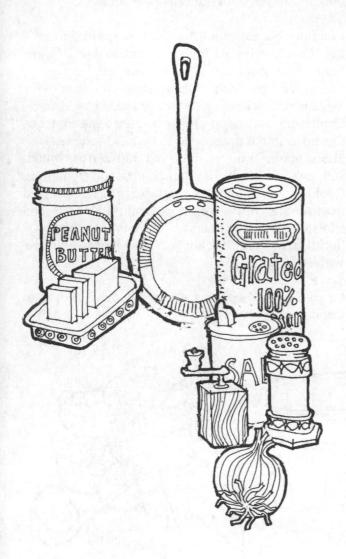

PEANUT BUTTER SOUP

2 tablespoons butter
2 tablespoons flour
1-1/2 pints milk

1 small onion, chopped
2 tablespoons grated Parmesan cheese
1/4 teaspoon celery seed
1/2 teaspoon salt
1/4 teaspoon black pepper
1 crumbled bay leaf
5 tablespoons peanut butter

macaroons (see below)

crisp-fried crumbled bacon or
chopped peanuts

Melt butter until bubbly, sprinkle with flour and
cook and stir 3 minutes. Gradually add milk; cook
and stir until smooth and slightly thickened.
Add onion, cheese, seasonings, bay leaf and peanut
butter. Cover, bring to boil and simmer 15 minutes.
Strain, adjust seasonings and ladle hot soup over
macaroons in 4 or 6 bowls. Sprinkle with crumbled
bacon or peanuts. Macaroons should stay crisp.
Serves 4 - 6
Or omit the macaroons, chill and serve in chilled
bowls; sprinkle with chopped peanuts.

MACAROONS

2 tablespoons softened butter
8 tablespoons grated almonds
8 tablespoons coarse dry breadcrumbs
1 tablespoon sugar
1 large egg, beaten

Combine ingredients and drop by teaspoonfuls into
hot fat. Cook until golden and crisp, drain on paper
towels and serve immediately.

CREAMY TAPIOCA SOUP

1/4 pint single cream
1/4 pint milk
4 tablespoons chopped leek
5 tablespoons chopped onion
1 garlic clove, finely chopped

2 pints rich chicken stock
5 tablespoons minute tapioca

1 egg yolk, beaten

1/8 teaspoon mace
1/4 teaspoon white pepper
1/2 teaspoon salt

1 ounce butter, finely diced
finely chopped chervil

Bring cream, milk, leeks, onion and garlic to boil and simmer 15 minutes. Strain and cool.

Bring stock to boil, gradually add tapioca, stirring constantly, and lower heat. Cover and cook 10 minutes.

Beat egg yolk and cooled cream, whisk in 1/4 pint hot soup and return to rest of soup. Reheat without boiling.

Season with mace, pepper and salt, adjusting to taste. Swirl in diced butter and sprinkle with finely chopped chervil.

Serves 6

Or omit diced butter. Just before serving add 4 tablespoons dry sherry.

GARLIC SOUP WITH POTATO BALLS

6 medium potatoes, peeled and quartered
1 small onion, chopped
1/2 teaspoon salt

5 garlic cloves (or more!), crushed
1/2 teaspoon salt
2 egg yolks, beaten
scant 1/2 pint olive oil

salt
black pepper
3 tablespoons flour

finely chopped parsley or
finely chopped fresh coriander

Garlic lovers: Here is an unusual flavor!

Boil potatoes and onion in salted water until soft. Drain, reserving liquid, and force potatoes through food mill or sieve.

Blend garlic, salt and egg yolks; gradually add oil, beating constantly. Combine with sieved potato and reserve 3/4 cup. Add remaining garlic-potato mixture to reserved potato water and blend well. Adjust seasonings with salt and pepper.

Mix reserved potato-garlic mixture with flour, adding more flour if needed to form small balls.

Return soup to boil, add balls, lower heat slightly and cook 5 minutes.

Garnish with finely chopped parsley or coriander.

Serves 6

Or season with a little vinegar.

CHEDDAR CHEESE VELOUTÉ

1-1/2 pints rich chicken stock
2 leeks, white only, chopped
6 - 8 tablespoons chopped onion
5 tablespoons chopped celery
6 parsley sprigs
1/2 teaspoon turmeric

3 tablespoons cornflour mixed with
3 tablespoons cold water
5 ounces sharp Cheddar cheese, grated
1/4 teaspoon each white pepper, paprika,
  and nutmeg

2 egg yolks, beaten
6 tablespoons double cream
scant 1/2 pint milk
5 tablespoons dry white wine

compound chili powder
salt

finely chopped chives
paprika

Bring stock, vegetables, parsley and turmeric to boil, cover and simmer 1 hour. Cool and strain.
Reheat, add cornflour-water binder, and cook and stir until smooth and slightly thickened.
Add cheese and seasonings and heat gently to melt cheese.
Beat yolks into cream, whisk in 1/4 pint hot soup, and return to rest of soup, together with milk. Reheat. Do not boil.
Add wine and adjust seasonings to taste with chili powder and salt.
Sprinkle with finely chopped chives and paprika, and serve with mushroom cornucopias. (See page 181).
Serves 6
Or garnish with generous amount of grated carrot.

MUSTARD SOUP

2 tablespoons each butter and flour
1 pint chicken stock
1/2 pint milk
1/2 teaspoon salt
1/4 teaspoon white pepper
1-1/2 teaspoons onion juice

2 egg yolks, beaten
3 tablespoons prepared mustard
3 tablespoons cream

whipped cream
finely chopped parsley

Melt butter until bubbly, sprinkle with flour, cook and stir 3 minutes. Gradually add stock and milk; cook and stir until smooth and slightly thickened. Season with salt, pepper and onion juice.
Combine yolks, mustard and cream. Whisk in 1/4 pint hot soup and return to rest of soup. Reheat; do not boil. Adjust seasonings to taste.
Garnish with dollops of whipped cream and finely chopped parsley.
Serves 4
Or add 1/4 pint double cream, chill, and serve in chilled bowls.

GAME BROTH WITH FORCEMEAT BALLS

2-1/2 pints stock made from any game

1 recipe forcemeat balls made from
 game used (see page 178)

6 fluid ounces double cream
1 egg yolk, beaten

finely chopped chervil
garlic croutons

Heat stock; beat cream and yolk and whisk in 1/4 pint hot stock. Return to rest of stock, reheat without boiling and add forcemeat balls cooked separately in salted water.
Garnish with finely chopped chervil and serve with garlic croutons.
Serves 6
Or omit the liaison of cream and egg; add 6 to 8 tablespoons dry red wine and 1 tablespoon red currant jelly.
Reheat.

PEANUT SOUP

2 teaspoons grated onion
6 - 8 tablespoons peanuts, ground
3 tablespoons butter
3 tablespoons flour
1-1/2 pints rich chicken stock

1 egg yolk, beaten
8 fluid ounces double cream

Tabasco
celery salt
white pepper
lemon juice

lemon slices
toasted peanuts

Sauté onion and peanuts in butter 5 minutes, stirring constantly. Sprinkle with flour, cook and stir 3 minutes, and gradually add stock. Cook and stir until smooth and slightly thickened; cover and simmer gently 15 to 20 minutes.
Combine yolk and cream, whisk in 1/4 pint hot soup, and return to rest of soup.
Season to taste with Tabasco, celery salt, white pepper and lemon juice; thin with more stock if desired. Reheat but do not boil.
Serve with lemon slices and extra toasted peanuts.
Serves 4 - 6
Or add 2 tablespoons each very finely chopped hot red pepper and green pepper the last few minutes of cooking.

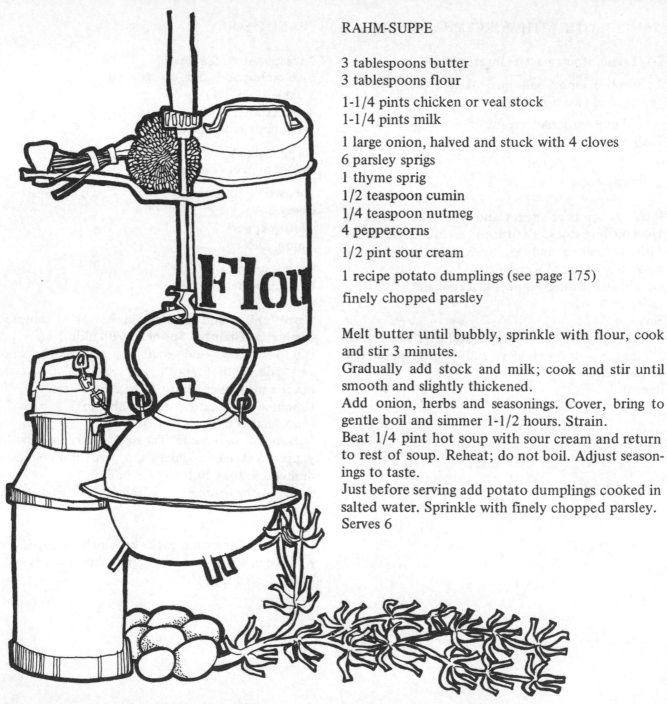

RAHM-SUPPE

3 tablespoons butter
3 tablespoons flour

1-1/4 pints chicken or veal stock
1-1/4 pints milk

1 large onion, halved and stuck with 4 cloves
6 parsley sprigs
1 thyme sprig
1/2 teaspoon cumin
1/4 teaspoon nutmeg
4 peppercorns

1/2 pint sour cream

1 recipe potato dumplings (see page 175)

finely chopped parsley

Melt butter until bubbly, sprinkle with flour, cook and stir 3 minutes.
Gradually add stock and milk; cook and stir until smooth and slightly thickened.
Add onion, herbs and seasonings. Cover, bring to gentle boil and simmer 1-1/2 hours. Strain.
Beat 1/4 pint hot soup with sour cream and return to rest of soup. Reheat; do not boil. Adjust seasonings to taste.
Just before serving add potato dumplings cooked in salted water. Sprinkle with finely chopped parsley.
Serves 6

MANDELSUPPE

3 ounces blanched almonds

1 tablespoon finely chopped onion
2 tablespoons butter
2 tablespoons flour
3/4 pint chicken stock

scant 1/2 pint evaporated milk

1/2 teaspoon salt
1/8 teaspoon white pepper
pure almond essence or
rose water

Grind almonds in blender.
Sauté onion in butter until butter bubbles. Sprinkle with flour, cook and stir 3 minutes and gradually add stock. Cook and stir until smooth and slightly thickened.
Add milk and almonds; cover and simmer 30 minutes.
Adjust seasonings to taste with salt, pepper and almond essence (be careful!) or rose water.
Serves 4
The consistency of this soup is gritty; if smoothness is preferred, simmer almonds in 1/2 pint stock, covered, for several hours to extract flavor. Force through sieve and add to rest of soup.

BIERSUPPE

4 teaspoons butter
1-1/2 tablespoons flour
2 tablespoons castor sugar

1-1/2 pints light beer
2 tablespoons lemon juice
1/2 teaspoon freshly grated lemon peel
1/8 teaspoon cinnamon

2 eggs, separated

cinnamon
tiny lemon peel strips

Melt butter until bubbly, sprinkle with flour and sugar, cook and stir until caramel colored.
Gradually add beer, cook and stir until smooth and slightly thickened. Add lemon juice, peel and cinnamon.
Beat egg yolks and whisk in 1/4 pint hot soup; return to rest of soup and reheat without boiling.
Whip egg whites and float on top with a dusting of cinnamon and lemon peel strips.
Serves 6

CZECH CABBAGE SOUP

1-1/2 pints chicken stock
1/2 pound cabbage, shredded
1 teaspoon caraway seeds
1-1/2 teaspoons instant onion
1/2 pint milk or 1/4 pint each single cream and
   milk

salt
pepper
caraway seeds
1/4 pound thin noodles, cooked

Combine stock, cabbage, caraway and onion, cover, bring to boil and simmer until cabbage is soft.
Purée in blender, reheat with milk or cream and milk, season to taste with salt and pepper and more caraway seeds. Add noodles, reheat and serve.
Serves 4 - 6

OTTO'S GRAPENUTS SOUP

4 onions, thinly sliced
2-1/2 pints rich beef stock

6 ounces grapenuts cereal
6 tablespoons grated Parmesan cheese
pinch nutmeg
2 tablespoons butter, melted

Cook onions in stock until tender.
Combine grapenuts, cheese and nutmeg; place in bottom of soup tureen.
Pour butter over and then the stock and onions.
Serve immediately—the grapenuts should stay crisp!
Serves 6

KULAJDA (CZECH)

3/4 pound mushrooms, thinly sliced
2 tablespoons each butter and olive oil
1/2 teaspoon each garlic powder, white
   pepper and oregano
1/4 teaspoon salt
dash cayenne pepper
1 teaspoon caraway seeds (optional)
2 teaspoons lemon juice

1-1/2 tablespoons flour
1 teaspoon paprika
3 tablespoons finely chopped parsley
1-1/4 pints stock

scant 1/2 pint sour cream
2 - 3 egg yolks, beaten

finely chopped fresh dill or
caraway seeds
paprika

Sauté mushrooms in butter and oil, seasoning while they are cooking with garlic powder, pepper, oregano, salt, cayenne, caraway and lemon juice, until mushrooms are golden.
Sprinkle with flour and paprika; cook and stir 3 minutes; add parsley and gradually add stock. Cook and stir until slightly thickened. Cover and simmer 15 minutes. Beat sour cream and egg yolks, whisk in 1/4 pint hot soup and return to rest of soup. Reheat without boiling and adjust seasonings to taste.
Sprinkle with dill or more caraway seeds (if used) and paprika. Serve with buttered pumpernickel squares topped with slices of mild Cheddar or other cheese.
Serves 4 - 6

BOGRACS GULYAS (HUNGARIAN)

4 strips bacon, diced
1 medium-sized onion, finely chopped

1 pound lean beef, cut into small cubes
1/2 teaspoon marjoram
1-1/2 teaspoons sharp Hungarian paprika
1 teaspoon salt
1 teaspoon caraway seed
1/4 teaspoon black pepper
1 garlic clove, very finely chopped
3 tablespoons tomato paste

2-1/2 pints rich beef stock

3/4 pound potatoes, peeled, diced and boiled
 until soft but firm

More than a thousand years ago Magyar shepherds carried supplies of cooked, dried meat cubes to turn their boiling pots of selected vegetables into delicious goulash soup. Hungarian goulash through the years has gained fame as a stew as well as a soup, but who can say where the border between them lies?

Sauté bacon and onion until onion is golden, stirring often. Push to side of pan.

Raise heat, add meat, cook and stir to brown, adding more bacon fat if needed. Sprinkle with seasonings and garlic, cook and stir 3 minutes, and blend in tomato paste.

Add stock, mix, cover and bring to boil. Simmer 40 minutes or until meat is tender.

Add potatoes, heat, adjust seasonings to taste and serve with an extra sprinkling of paprika.

Serves 6 - 8

Or can also add cubed, cooked carrots, celery and green pepper.

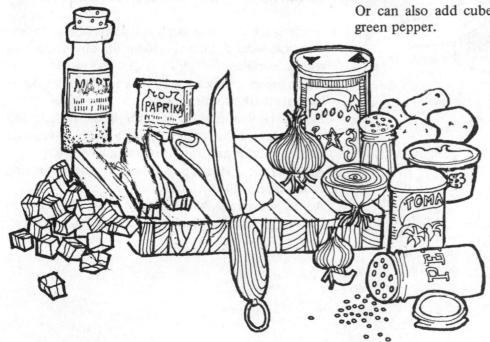

CURRIED LAMB SOUP

3/4 pound lean stewing lamb,
 cut into 1/2- to 3/4-inch cubes
3/4 pint water

1 onion, chopped
4 tablespoons chopped green pepper (optional)
2 to 3 teaspoons curry powder
1/2 teaspoon paprika
1 1/2 tablespoons butter
1-1/4 pints lamb stock
1 large ripe tomato, peeled and chopped
salt, pepper and cayenne pepper to taste
4 tablespoons raw white rice, well washed
1 large tart eating apple, peeled, cored and
 chopped
4 tablespoons sultanas or raisins

1 small ripe but firm banana, peeled and sliced

In soup pot combine lamb and water. Bring to boil
and boil 4 to 5 minutes. Skim off any scum that
rises to surface.
Sauté onion, pepper, curry powder and paprika in
butter, stirring to blend well, 3 to 5 minutes.
Add to lamb and water with the stock, tomato and
seasonings. Bring to boil, lower heat, cover and
simmer 1 hour or until meat is almost tender.
Add rice, and simmer 15 minutes. Add apple and
sultanas and simmer another 5 minutes.
Adjust seasonings and spices to taste. Transfer to
4 heated soup bowls and garnish with banana slices.
Serves 4

RUSSIAN CABBAGE SOUP

1/2 pound each cubed beef and lean pork
1/4 pound diced salt pork

1 small cabbage, finely shredded
2 large tomatoes, peeled and diced
1 medium-sized onion, diced
1 bay leaf
1/4 teaspoon pepper
1/2 teaspoon salt
1-1/2 pints beef stock made with short ribs
 and marrow bones

for garnish:

grated Parmesan cheese or
crisp-fried crumbled bacon
sour cream

Sauté beef, pork and salt pork to brown slightly.
Add half the cabbage and add remaining ingredients
except garnish. Cover, bring to boil and simmer
1-1/2 hours or until meat is tender. Remove bay
leaf.
Bring to boil, add rest of cabbage and cook until
tender-crisp.
Serve with grated Parmesan cheese, or sprinkle with
crumbled bacon and serve with a bowl of sour cream.
Serves 4 - 6
Or cook diced potatoes and/or celeriac in soup
10 minutes before adding cabbage.

CHLODNIK (POLISH)

1 garlic clove
1/4 teaspoon salt
2 - 3 cucumbers, peeled, seeded and
 finely diced
1 pound beetroots, boiled, peeled
 and finely chopped
4 tablespoons very finely chopped celery
1/2 pint milk or 1/4 pint each single cream
 and milk
1-1/2 pints sour cream
3 tablespoons finely chopped parsley
2 tablespoons finely chopped chives

salt
pepper

julienne strips of beetroots and cucumber
sliced radishes

Chop garlic finely and crush with salt; combine with
cucumbers, beetroots and celery. Beat milk, or
cream and milk, with sour cream and combine with
parsley, chives, and cucumber-beetroot mixture.
Add salt and pepper to taste, chill and adjust seasonings to taste.
Serve with garnish of beetroot and cucumber
julienne strips, and sliced radishes.
Serves 4 - 6

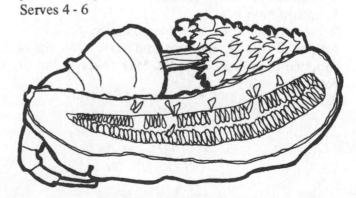

MIDDLE EAST YOGHURT SOUP

6 - 8 tablespoons pearl barley
3/4 pint water

1-1/2 pints cold water
3/4 pint yoghurt (homemade is best)

4 eggs
2 tablespoons flour
2 tablespoons finely chopped onion
2 tablespoons butter
salt

juice from 1 large lemon

finely chopped mint
finely chopped fresh coriander

It will not surprise me if this soup, suggested by a friend, does not appeal to every palate. Half the fun of exploring soups is trying the strange ones. After all, there are acquired tastes.

Cook barley in 3/4 pint water 1 hour, adding more water if needed. Drain.
Combine cold water and yoghurt. Beat eggs and flour and combine with yoghurt. Bring slowly to simmer and cook 3 minutes.
Add barley, onions, butter and salt to taste; simmer 1 more minute.
Remove from heat and add lemon juice.
Adjust seasonings to taste and serve with finely chopped mint and coriander. May be served hot or cold.
Serves 8

AVGOLEMONO

1-1/2 tablespoons cornflour
1/2 pint single cream
1/2 pint milk
1-1/2 pints slightly gelatinous rich chicken stock

6 egg yolks, beaten
1/4 teaspoon paprika
1/8 teaspoon cayenne pepper
about 1/2 pint lemon juice
salt
pepper

thin lemon slices
finely chopped parsley and/or chives
sieved hard-boiled eggs

Mix cornflour with a little of the cream, add to rest of cream. Add cream and milk to stock, cook and stir until smooth and slightly thickened.
Whisk 1/4 pint hot soup into egg yolks. Return to rest of soup, beating constantly, and add paprika, cayenne and lemon juice. Adjust seasonings with salt and pepper to taste, strain through fine sieve and chill thoroughly.
Serve in chilled bowls with a garnish of thinly sliced lemon, finely chopped parsley and/or chives, and sieved hard-boiled eggs.
Serves 6
Or heat but do not boil. Add 1 teaspoon grated lemon rind and fold in the beaten whites of two eggs. Serve over hot rice.

BORSCHT

*Borscht – Borsch – Borsht – Borschdt – Borshch:
More varied by far in its forms than in its spellings.
Older recipes—and some new—call for Hamburg
parsley, which seems to be unavailable in most
shops. The one I dug from my garden offered
nothing worthwhile.*

TOMATO BORSHCH (RUSSIAN)

1 medium-sized onion, chopped
2 tablespoons butter

3/4 pint tomato juice
1/2 pint rich brown beef stock
1/2 teaspoon each citric acid and sugar

1 small head cabbage, finely shredded
3 ounces cooked meat, preferably
  from stock bones, shredded

black pepper
sour cream

Sauté onion in butter until soft and slightly
browned.
Add tomato juice, stock, citric acid and sugar. Cover,
bring to boil and simmer 30 minutes. Strain.
Bring back to boil, add cabbage and cook until
tender-crisp. Reheat with meat and adjust seasoning to taste with more citric acid and/or sugar.
Sprinkle with black pepper and serve with a bowl
of sour cream.
Serves 3 - 4

COLD CLEAR BORSCHT

3/4 pound raw beetroots, peeled and grated
3 tablespoons grated onion and juice
water to cover (about 1 pint)
1 teaspoon each citric acid and sugar

1 egg, well beaten

salt
black pepper

sour cream
finely chopped chives

Combine beetroots, onion, water, citric acid and
sugar.
Cover, bring to boil and simmer 30 minutes.
Whisk 1/4 pint hot soup into egg, return to rest of
soup, cook and stir 3 minutes. Do not boil.
Strain, chill and adjust seasonings with salt and pepper. Serve in chilled bowls garnished with dollops of
sour cream and finely chopped chives.
Serves 3 - 4

COLD RUSSIAN BORSHCH

3/4 pint tomato juice
3 spring onions and tops, finely chopped
  and crushed with 1/2 teaspoons salt and
  2 tablespoons sour cream
1 pound beetroots, cooked, peeled and slivered
1 cucumber, peeled, seeded and slivered
2 hard-boiled eggs, sliced
6 radishes, thinly sliced

salt
black pepper

for garnish:
finely chopped fresh dill
sour cream

Spectacular to behold! Typical of the grand manner of the Russian expatriate from whom it came.

Blend 1/4 pint tomato juice with the spring onion-salt-sour cream mixture and combine with rest of ingredients.
Chill and adjust seasonings with salt and pepper.
Serve in chilled bowls with a generous sprinkling of finely chopped fresh dill and a bowl of sour cream.
Serves 6
Cooked prawns may be added.

EASY RUSSIAN BORSHCH

1-1/2 pounds brisket of beef or
  meaty, lean short ribs
1 medium-sized onion, chopped
1 bay leaf
1 teaspoon salt
6 peppercorns
2-1/2 pints water

1 pound raw beetroots, peeled and
  coarsely grated
2 large carrots, coarsely grated
1 large potato, peeled and diced
8 ounces tomato purée
3/4 pound cabbage, thinly shredded

finely chopped parsley
sour cream

Combine beef, onion, bay leaf, salt, peppercorns and water. Cover, bring to boil and simmer 3 hours. Strain, cool and chill to remove fat.
Bring stock to boil, add beetroots, carrots, potatoes and tomato purée. Cook 10 minutes. Add cabbage, bring back to boil, and cook until tender-crisp. Adjust seasonings with salt and pepper and sprinkle with finely chopped parsley. Serve with a bowl of sour cream.
Serves 6
Or season with red-wine vinegar and sugar to taste. Add diced meat, if heavier soup is desired.

CRIMEAN BORSHCH

4 tablespoons finely chopped parsley
1 chopped carrot
1 chopped onion
2 chopped leeks, white only
1/2 pound lean salt pork, diced
3 tablespoons butter and/or rendered beef fat

1-1/2 pounds beef brisket or meaty,
  lean short ribs, cut up
3-1/4 pints water

6 peppercorns
1 bay leaf
1 teaspoon salt

6 beetroots, shredded
1 carrot, shredded
2 potatoes, diced
6 - 8 tablespoons shredded swedes and/or
  white turnips

3/4 pound cabbage, finely shredded
6 ounces or more reserved meat
1 teaspoon each citric acid and sugar
1/4 teaspoon black pepper

2 beetroots, shredded

finely chopped fresh dill
sour cream

Sauté parsley, vegetables and salt pork in butter and/or fat until golden. Add meat, water, peppercorns, bay leaf and salt. Cover, bring to boil and simmer 2 hours. Strain, reserve and dice meat; set aside. Chill stock and remove fat.

Bring stock to boil, add beetroots, carrot, potatoes and swedes or turnips. Simmer 10 minutes. Add cabbage and reserved meat, bring to boil and cook 5 minutes. Add citric acid, sugar and pepper. Adjust to taste.
Wrap additional 2 shredded beetroots in cheesecloth and squeeze out as much juice as possible. Add juice only to soup for color.
Reheat and serve sprinkled with lots of fresh dill. Serve with a bowl of sour cream.
Serves 10
Or 8 ounces tomato purée may be added for different flavor.

A Meal in a Bowl

Drink's bad effects may in a great measure be taken off by a dinner of mutton broth, or soup maigre, on the following day.
—A. Hunter, "Culina," 1806

Boisterous, medieval knights clutching dripping chunks of meat from a giant bowl may come to mind when thinking of soup as a complete meal. Generally these hearty soups contain chunks of solid food and therefore should be served in broad, shallow bowls with knives and forks as well as spoons.

French bread and unsalted butter make ideal accompaniments. Small salads and light desserts go well with these soups, too.

SEAFOOD & CHICKEN GUMBO

1 2-pound chicken, cut up
2 tablespoons butter and/or rendered chicken fat
3-1/4 pints chicken stock
1 teaspoon paprika
2 garlic cloves
6 - 8 tablespoons chopped celery leaves
1/2 teaspoon turmeric
1/4 pound lean ham, cubed
1 stalk celery, diced
1 bunch spring onions and tops, chopped
1 leek, chopped
2 tablespoons butter and/or fat
2 tablespoons flour
1/2 teaspoon pepper
1 teaspoon paprika
bouquet garni of:
  8 sprigs parsley
  1 sprig thyme
  1 bay leaf
  4 cloves
2 blades mace or 6 allspice berries
1/4 pound flaked crab
1/4 pound fresh or frozen prawns
1/2 pound scallops, poached and sliced
1/2 pound okra, cut up and cooked

salt
pepper
Worcestershire sauce
Tabasco

1 teaspoon filé*

finely chopped parsley
paprika

*see glossary

Brown chicken in butter and/or fat, add stock, paprika, garlic, celery leaves and turmeric. Cover, bring to boil and simmer gently 1 hour or until chicken is tender. Cool, remove chicken from bones, cut up, and reserve. Strain stock.

Brown ham, celery, green onions and leek in butter or fat. Sprinkle with flour, cook and stir 3 minutes, and deglaze with 3/4 pint of the stock, scraping the bottom of pan. Add rest of stock, pepper, paprika, and bouquet garni. Cover and simmer 1 hour.

Discard bouquet garni. Add crab, prawns, scallops, okra and reserved chicken. Reheat carefully and adjust seasonings to taste with salt, pepper, Worcestershire sauce and Tabasco. Remove from heat, stir in filé, and sprinkle with finely chopped parsley and paprika. Serve with garlic Fench bread.

Serves 8 - 10

Or add 1 pound tomatoes, peeled and stewed. Serve with bowls of fluffy white rice.

131

LEEK AND BARLEY SOUP

2 pounds leeks, white part and some of
 tender green, finely chopped
2-1/2 pints chicken stock

1 tablespoon rendered chicken fat
6 - 8 tablespoons pearl barley, cooked in salted
 water 1-1/2 hours

8 - 10 ounces cooked chicken, shredded
1/4 pint single cream
1/4 pint milk

salt
white pepper

finely chopped parsley

Cook leeks in half of the stock until tender.
Add fat, drained barley and rest of stock. Cover and
cook until barley is mushy.
Add chicken, cream and milk, and reheat.
Adjust seasonings with salt and pepper and sprinkle
with lots of finely chopped parsley.
Serves 6

HERB OXTAIL SOUP

2-1/2 pounds oxtails, cut up
2 tablespoons butter and/or rendered beef fat
1/2 teaspoon salt
1 teaspoon white pepper

1 medium-sized onion, chopped
2 garlic cloves, finely chopped
1/4 pound mushrooms and stems, chopped
1-1/4 pints dry red wine
3/4 pint water
bouquet garni of:
  2 sprigs parsley
  1 sprig rosemary
  1 sprig thyme
  2 sprigs oregano or marjoram

6 - 8 tablespoons pearl barley

2 large carrots, sliced
1 large potato, peeled and diced
1 pint beef stock

6 - 8 tablespoons Madeira

Brown oxtails in butter and/or fat on all sides, sprinkling with salt and pepper as they are cooking.
Add onion, garlic and mushrooms the last turn, brown and add wine, water and bouquet garni. Cover, bring to boil and cook 1-1/2 hours.
Cool, chill, remove fat and bring back to boil. Add barley and cook 1-1/2 hours.
Remove bouquet garni, add carrots, potato, and beef stock. Bring back to boil and cook 15 minutes or until vegetables are soft but not mushy. Adjust seasonings.
Just before serving add 6 to 8 tablespoons Madeira or to taste.
Serves 4 - 6

THICK OXTAIL SOUP

2-1/2 pounds oxtails, cut up
1 medium-sized onion, chopped
3 garlic cloves, finely chopped
2 stalks celery, chopped
1 teaspoon salt
3 pints water

6 - 8 tablespoons pearl barley

6 - 8 tablespoons brown lentils

salt
black pepper

finely chopped parsley

Combine oxtails, vegetables, salt and water; cover, bring to boil and cook 1-1/2 hours at medium-high boil. Skim off any scum that rises to the surface.
Cool, chill and defat. Reheat, add barley and cook rapidly 45 minutes, adding water if needed as the barley swells.
Add lentils and cook another 45 minutes until barley and lentils are tender but lentils still hold their shape. Add water if the soup is too thick, reheat, adjust seasonings with salt and pepper and serve with a generous sprinkling of finely chopped parsley.
Serves 4 - 6

SPLIT PEA SOUP

1/2 pound green and/or yellow split peas

3 - 4 ham hocks and/or bones with meat
1 pair pig's trotters
2 medium-sized onions, sliced
2 large carrots, chopped
2 garlic cloves, finely chopped
4 stalks celery and leaves, chopped
2 tablespoons butter and/or ham fat

12 peppercorns
3 parsley sprigs
1 bay leaf
2 teaspoons mixed diced herbs
2-1/2 pints water and juice from canned ham and/or
  chicken stock

1 can evaporated milk

marjoram
salt
pepper

dry sherry

Brown ham hocks and/or bones, pig's trotters and vegetables in butter and/or fat.

Add peas, peppercorns, herbs and water, juice and/or stock. Cover, bring to boil and simmer, stirring occasionally, 3 hours. Remove ham hock and pig's trotters.

Force through food mill or sieve, pushing as much pulp through as possible. Reheat with evaporated milk, thin with stock if desired, and adjust seasonings with marjoram, salt and pepper.

Just before serving add dry sherry to taste and serve with thin slices of rye bread.

Serves 6 - 8

For heartier meal, add meat from ham hocks, cooked sausages, browned mushrooms, diced potatoes and/or julienne strips of vegetable. Sprinkle with grated Parmesan cheese.

BOUILLABAISSE

1 small onion, finely chopped
4 tablespoons finely chopped white of leeks
6 garlic cloves, finely chopped
1 sprig fennel (if available)
3 sprigs crushed parsley
1 bay leaf
1 3-inch strip of (dried) orange peel

5 - 6 pounds (bought weight) of fresh seafood, some from each of the following categories:

crustaceans	firm	delicate
crab	sea bass	whiting
prawns	cod	red mullet
crawfish	haddock	John Dory
lobster	grey mullet	sole
	sea trout	plaice
	rock salmon	lemon sole
	halibut	
	turbot	
	eel	

about 1/4 pint olive oil
1 teaspoon salt
1/4 teaspoon freshly ground black pepper
1/4 teaspoon powdered saffron

5 pints water, fish stock and/or dry white wine — combination of

10 - 12 stale French bread slices (not toasted or fried)

Described by Thackeray in "The Ballad of Bouillabaisse" as "a noble dish—a sort of soup, or broth, or brew" a bouillabaisse is a general category more than a particular soup.

Put vegetables, herbs and orange peel in a large pot. Arrange selected cleaned crustaceans over vegetables and top with firm fish of choice. Pour olive oil over and sprinkle with salt, pepper and saffron. Add liquid, cover, and bring to fast boil; quick cooking is essential to the consistency. Boil 7 minutes, add delicate fish of choice and cook 6 more minutes. Do not cook more than 15 minutes in all. Place a slice of bread in each bowl. Arrange crustaceans and fish on a platter to be served separately. Adjust flavor of broth and moisten each piece of bread. Serve rest of broth in tureen. Serve with aioli sauce (see page 179), if desired.
Serves 10 - 12
Quartered or sliced potatoes may be added at the same time as the firm fish.

EAST INDIAN MULLIGATAWNY

1 2-1/2 to 3-pound chicken, cut up
1 teaspoon paprika
1/2 teaspoon salt
1/4 teaspoon black pepper
3 - 4 tablespoons rendered chicken fat

5 tablespoons each diced turnip, carrot, onion,
  celery and tart peeled eating apple

1 tablespoon rice flour
1 - 2 teaspoons curry powder

2-1/2 pints chicken stock
bouquet garni of:
  1 bay leaf
  3 parsley sprigs
  1 thyme sprig
  6 peppercorns
  2 whole cloves
4 tablespoons finely chopped green pepper
1/8 teaspoon mace
1/4 teaspoon black pepper
1 teaspoon salt
4 - 8 tablespoons tomato paste (optional)
1/4 teaspoon sugar (optional)
lemon rice balls (see opposite)

Sprinkle chicken with paprika, salt and pepper and sauté a few pieces at a time in fat. Remove and set aside.

Add vegetables and apple; stir and cook until golden.

Sprinkle with flour and curry powder, cook and stir 3 minutes, gradually add stock, and cook and stir until smooth. Add chicken, bouquet garni, green pepper and seasonings. Cover, bring to boil and simmer until chicken is tender.

Remove chicken and cut meat into small pieces. Set aside.

Strain broth, forcing as much pulp through sieve as possible.

Heat, adjust seasonings and add tomato paste and sugar if desired.

Serve with lemon rice balls and as much chicken as desired.

Serves 6

Or add puréed canned chick peas and combine thoroughly.

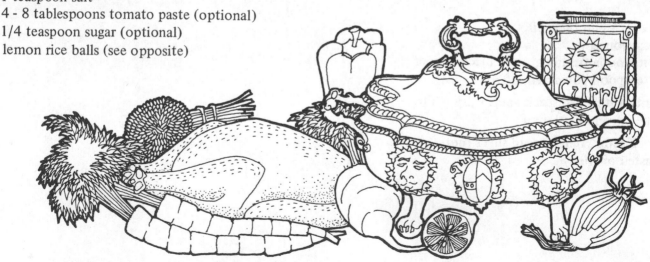

136

LEMON RICE BALLS

3/4 cup (4-1/2 ounces) raw long-grain rice,
 well washed
1-1/2 cups plus 2 tablespoons water
1-1/2 tablespoons lemon juice

1/2 teaspoon freshly grated lemon peel
1/2 teaspoon salt
1/4 teaspoon black pepper

2 - 3 tablespoons garlic olive oil
 (let 2 or 3 garlic cloves stand in 1/2 pint olive
 oil overnight — keep on hand!)

Spread rice evenly on the bottom of a saucepan; combine water and lemon juice and add to rice. Let stand at least 1 hour. Bring to boil over high heat, uncovered, and reduce heat slightly. Cook until all the water has evaporated. Cover immediately and cook at lowest heat 30 to 40 minutes. Rice should be sticky but not gooey.

Season with lemon peel, salt and pepper, stirring in with a fork. Adjust seasonings to taste.

When cool enough to handle, form rice into 30 marble-size balls; if it cools off too much you may need to dip your fingers in water. These may be made ahead and kept at room temperature up to 4 hours. Sauté balls in oil, turning several times, until they barely start to turn golden. Do not sauté too long or they will form too much crust. Drain on paper towels and serve immediately.

CREAMY MINESTRONE WITH PESTO

2 tablespoons finely chopped onion
1 stalk celery, finely chopped
2 teaspoons olive oil
2 turnips and tops, finely chopped
2 ounces cabbage, finely shredded
2 ounces beetroot greens, stems and ribs
  removed (or Swiss chard), finely shredded
4 tablespoons finely chopped parsley
1/2 teaspoon salt
1/4 teaspoon black pepper
1-1/4 pints rich veal or chicken stock
1/2 pint milk
1/4 pint single cream
1 recipe pesto (see below)
salt
pepper
oregano

grated Parmesan cheese

Sauté onion and celery in oil until soft. Add vegetables, parsley, salt, pepper and stock. Cover, bring to boil and simmer 20 minutes until vegetables are tender. Add milk and cream, reheat and adjust seasonings to taste with salt, pepper and oregano.

Just before serving drizzle pesto over top. Serve with Parmesan cheese.

Serves 6

PESTO

4 tablespoons finely chopped fresh basil
1 garlic clove, finely chopped
8 tablespoons freshly grated Parmesan cheese
1 tablespoon olive oil

Mash basil, garlic and cheese; add oil as needed to make a paste.

LAMB WITH MINT

3-1/2 to 4 pounds neck of lamb
1/2 pint dry red wine
generous 2 pints water
1 onion stuck with 3 cloves
bouquet garni of:
  4 parsley sprigs
  2 summer savory sprigs
  1 thyme sprig
  1 bay leaf
  6 peppercorns
2 stalks celery and tops, chopped
3 parsnips, diced
2 teaspoons salt
2 - 3 ounces celeriac, diced
8 - 10 ounces frozen peas
2 tablespoons finely chopped leek

salt

pepper

6 - 8 tablespoons finely chopped fresh mint

A rich luncheon or supper soup to be served in small portions.

Combine lamb with wine, water, onion, bouquet garni, celery, parsnips and salt. Cover, bring to boil and cook 3 hours until lamb is tender. Remove lamb and cut off enough meat to make 1/2 to 3/4 pound. Reserve.
Strain stock, cool and chill to remove fat.
Bring back to boil with celeriac, peas and leeks, cover and simmer 15 minutes or until vegetables are soft. Purée in blender.
Add slivered lamb, reheat and adjust seasonings with salt and pepper.
Sprinkle with mint, bring *just* to boil and serve immediately.
Serves 6

WINTER VEGETABLE BROTH

1-3/4 pints lamb or veal stock
leftover lamb and bones
3/4 pint water
5 ounces pearl barley

1 small turnip, diced
2 small carrots, diced
1 leek, white and some green
  top, finely chopped
2 stalks celery, diced

1/4 pound mushrooms, diced
3 large tomatoes, peeled and diced

salt

pepper

This is a simple, rather bland soup. Serve with a tangy salad and crisp rolls.

Combine stock, leftover lamb and bones, water and barley. Cover, bring to boil and simmer 1/2 hour. Remove meat and bones, shred meat and reserve.
Continue cooking soup 1-1/2 hours or until barley is soft.
Add turnip, carrots, leek and celery; cook 15 minutes. Add mushrooms and tomatoes and cook 5 more minutes. Add shredded lamb and reheat. Adjust seasonings to taste with salt and pepper. Soup should be thick.
Serves 6 - 8

SLUMGULLION

1 veal knuckle, blanched
2 large, meaty veal shanks, blanched
3-1/4 pints water
1 teaspoon salt
bouquet garni of:
  4 parsley sprigs
  1 marjoram sprig
  1 rosemary sprig
  1 thyme sprig
  1 tablespoon basil
  1 stalk celery, cut up
1 onion stuck with 3 cloves

4 tablespoons each finely chopped onion
  and celery
2 tablespoons finely chopped green pepper
1 garlic clove, finely chopped
2 tablespoons olive oil
4 - 5 ounces each diced turnips and carrots
2 ounces diced celeriac
3 ounces green beans, cut on diagonal
1/4 pound spicy dry continental sausage, sliced

1 small potato, peeled and diced

4 - 6 ounces frozen peas, thawed
4 - 6 ounces frozen spinach, thawed
1 can (14-ounce) peeled tomatoes
1 pint rich beef stock
6 - 8 ounces veal (from shanks), cubed

4 ounces pasta shells, cooked

garlic powder
crumbled basil
salt
pepper

grated Parmesan cheese

Combine veal knuckle, shanks, water, salt, bouquet garni and onion. Cover, bring to boil and simmer 1-1/2 to 2 hours until veal is tender.
Remove shanks and cut meat into cubes; reserve. Strain and cool stock, chill and remove fat.
Sauté onion, celery, green pepper and garlic in oil until soft. Add to stock, bring to boil and add turnips, carrots, celeriac, beans and sausage.
Bring back to boil and cook 10 minutes.
Add potatoes and cook 5 minutes. Add peas, spinach, tomatoes, stock and reserved meat cubes.
Bring to boil and boil 5 minutes; add pasta, reheat and adjust seasonings to taste with garlic powder, basil, salt and pepper.
Serve with hot French rolls, unsalted butter and a robust red wine. Pass round a bowl of grated Parmesan cheese.
Serves 8 - 10
Just before serving add red wine to taste.

CREAM OF CHICKEN WITH VEGETABLES

1 2-1/2 to 3 pound chicken
3/4 pint beef stock
1-1/2 pints chicken stock
1 onion stuck with 3 cloves
1 chopped leek
1 chopped carrot
2 stalks chopped celery
3 chopped spring onions and tops
1 sprig each marjoram and thyme
3 parsley sprigs
1 tablespoon salt
6 peppercorns

4 tablespoons each cooked peas, corn, mushrooms
  and cauliflower
3 egg yolks, beaten
1/2 pint double cream
1/4 pint milk
1/2 teaspoon salt
1/4 teaspoon white pepper
1 tablespoon lemon juice
1/4 teaspoon tarragon

grated Cheddar cheese or raw carrot

Combine chicken, stocks, vegetables, herbs, salt and peppercorns. Cover, bring to boil and simmer 1 hour or until chicken is tender. Remove chicken and cool. Strain broth, cool, and chill to remove fat.

Remove meat from chicken, cut 12 ounces white meat into strips and reserve. Dice 8 ounces dark meat and purée in blender with 1/2 pint stock. Return to rest of stock and reheat.

Beat yolks and double cream, whisk in 1/4 pint hot soup and return to rest of soup. Add vegetables and chicken white meat. Reheat but do not boil.

Thin soup down to taste with milk, season with salt, pepper, lemon juice and tarragon. Adjust seasoning to taste and serve with a garnish of grated Cheddar cheese or grated raw carrot.

Be sure to stir well when serving, as puréed dark meat tends to settle on the bottom.
Serves 6 - 8

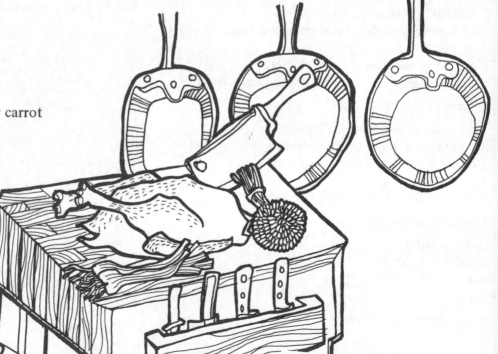

VEAL SOUP PROVENÇALE

2 tablespoons olive oil
2 tablespoons flour

1-1/2 pints rich chicken or veal stock

1 large onion, chopped
1 teaspoon finely chopped garlic
generous pinch celery seed
1-1/2 pounds lean veal, cut in 1/2-inch cubes
1/2 teaspoon Maggi
1/2 teaspoon salt
1/2 teaspoon white pepper
1 egg yolk, beaten
2 - 3 tablespoons lemon juice

finely chopped parsley and/or grated Parmesan

Heat oil, sprinkle with flour, cook and stir 3 minutes. Gradually add stock; cook and stir until smooth and slightly thickened.
Add onion, garlic, veal and seasonings. Cover and simmer 30 minutes or until veal is tender.
Adjust seasonings to taste.
Beat egg yolk and lemon juice, whisk in 1/4 pint hot soup and return to rest of soup. Serve immediately sprinkled with finely chopped parsley and/or grated Parmesan.
Serves 4
Or add 4 ounces cooked small shell macaroni and/or a scant 1/2 pint double cream.

TURKEY SOUP WITH OYSTERS

4 stalks celery, sliced on diagonal
6 - 8 tablespoons each diced onion and leeks
1 garlic clove, finely chopped
4 tablespoons butter and/or rendered chicken fat

5 tablespoons flour

3/4 pint creamy milk
1-1/4 pints rich turkey stock

12 ounces leftover turkey, diced
1/2 teaspoon each nutmeg and white pepper
1/2 teaspoon salt
1 teaspoon lemon juice

12 oysters
1 tablespoon butter

finely chopped parsley

Sauté celery, onion, leeks and garlic in butter and/or fat until onions are soft.
Sprinkle with flour, cook and stir 3 minutes, and gradually add creamy milk and stock. Cook and stir until smooth and thickened.
Add turkey, reheat and season with nutmeg, pepper, salt and lemon juice. Adjust to taste.
Frizzle oysters and their juice in butter until edges curl. Add to hot soup and serve immediately with a generous sprinkling of finely chopped parsley.
Serves 6
Very finely chopped raw celery and leaves also enhance the flavor; sprinkle on top.

MENUDO

2 pounds honeycomb tripe
1 veal knuckle
3/4 pounds chickpeas, soaked overnight

4 pints water
1 garlic clove
1/2 teaspoon oregano
3 spring onions, cut up
6 peppercorns
1/2 bunch coriander stems only, cut up
1/2 teaspoon compound chili powder
1 teaspoon salt

coriander sprigs for garnish

*Be prepared for something out of the ordinary.
Smooth tripe, which is chewier, may be preferred;
it takes 1/2 hour more cooking.*

Blanch tripe and veal knuckle separately.
Cut tripe into 1-inch pieces and set aside.
Combine veal knuckle and remaining ingredients
except chickpeas. Cover, bring to boil and simmer
1 hour. Add chickpeas and simmer for a further
hour. Add tripe, bring back to boil and cook
another hour. Adjust seasonings.
Garnish with coriander sprigs.
Serves 10 - 12

ITALIAN BREAD AND CABBAGE SOUP

8 slices stale French or Italian bread
2-1/2 pints rich beef stock
3-5 garlic cloves, crushed
6 ounces cabbage, finely shredded
1 small onion, thinly sliced
scant 1/2 pint tomato sauce
1/2 teaspoon salt
1/4 teaspoon black pepper
6 tablespoons grated Parmesan cheese
finely chopped flat leaf parsley

Cover the bottom of a large heavy casserol (with
a tight lid) with bread, overlapping the slices. Pour
in stock and cover with a layer of garlic, cabbage
and onion. Spread with tomato sauce and season
with salt, pepper and cheese.
Cover and bake in a 375°F/Mark 5/190°C oven 45
minutes. Check after 30 minutes and add extra stock
if the soup appears to be too thick.
Serve with a generous sprinkling of finely chopped
parsley.
Serves 4 - 6

BOURRIDE

2 pounds firm white fish fillets
3-1/4 pints water
2 small onions, chopped
2 large tomatoes, chopped
3 parsley sprigs
1 oregano or marjoram sprig
1 bay leaf
6 coriander seeds
2 stalks celery, chopped
3 garlic cloves
1 strip orange peel or 1 teaspoon grated dried
   orange peel
2 teaspoons salt
4 peppercorns
1/4 teaspoon saffron
2 tablespoons olive oil

8 slices stale French bread

salt
black pepper

2 egg yolks, beaten

aioli sauce (see page 179)

Bring water, vegetables, herbs, seasonings and oil to boil, cover and simmer 20 minutes.

Raise heat, add fish wrapped in cheesecloth, lower heat and poach gently 10 to 12 minutes until just tender.

Place a slice of bread in each of 8 bowls, top with half a fish fillet, and keep warm.

Strain stock and adjust seasonings with salt and pepper.

Whisk 1/4 pint hot soup into egg yolks and return to rest of soup.

Ladle soup into bowls and top with 1 tablespoon aioli sauce for each serving.

Serves 8 generously

FAMILY MINESTRONE

2-1/2 pints stock made with oxtails or leftover
 roast beef
4 tablespoons chopped flat leaf parsley
1/8 teaspoon rosemary

4 tablespoons finely chopped leek
8 tablespoons finely chopped onion
1 tablespoon olive oil
1 16-ounce can kidney beans, drained and rinsed

2 - 3 stalks Swiss chard, cut up
2 ounces each broad beans, green beans,
 cut up, broccoli flowerets, diced potato and
 chopped celery
12 ounces cabbage, finely shredded

6 - 8 tablespoons soup pasta
1/2 - 3/4 pint tomato juice or
 vegetable juice
6 - 8 tablespoons pearl barley, precooked
6 - 8 ounces diced meat from bones

salt
pepper
6 - 8 tablespoons dry sherry

finely chopped flat leaf parsley
very finely chopped garlic
grated Parmesan cheese

Simmer stock with parsley and rosemary 20 minutes. Strain.

Sauté leeks and onion in oil 5 minutes. Add to reheated stock with beans and fresh vegetables. Bring to boil and cook until vegetables are almost tender.

Add pasta, cook until tender and reheat with tomato juice or vegetable juice, barley and meat.

Adjust seasonings to taste with salt and pepper, add sherry just before serving and sprinkle with lots of parsley and garlic. Serve with grated Parmesan.

Serves 6 - 8

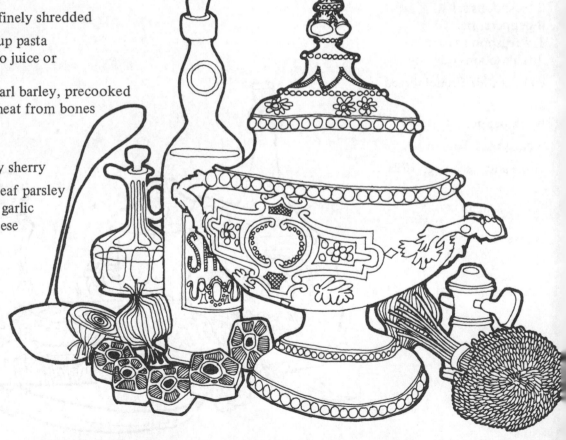

STUFFED SQUID SPECTACULAR

6 squid (5- or 6-inch)

2 tablespoons finely chopped onion
1 teaspoon finely chopped garlic
1 tablespoon finely chopped dried mushrooms
  which have first been softened in lukewarm water
  and patted dry

2 tablespoons olive oil

1-1/2 tablespoons very finely chopped parsley
6 - 8 tablespoons fine bread crumbs
1 tablespoon grated Parmesan cheese
1/4 teaspoon oregano
1/2 teaspoon salt
1/4 teaspoon black pepper

8 tablespoons finely chopped celery and leaves
4 tablespoons thinly sliced carrot
4 tablespoons finely chopped onion
1 garlic clove, finely chopped
3 tablespoons finely chopped parsley
3 tablespoons olive oil

2 large tomatoes, peeled and diced
1 teaspoon anchovy paste

6 - 8 tablespoons white wine

1-1/4 pints fish stock
1/2 pint chicken stock

12 ounces firm white fish, cut into
  2-inch cubes

salt
pepper
Tabasco

Clean squid as follows. Holding tail end and head firmly, pull fins and outer tail covering from head and tentacles. Remove the silvery grey ink sac from the inner tail section and discard it. Cut tentacles from head section with a sharp knife, just beyond the eyes. Discard eye section, innards and cartilage from base of tentacle section. Remove and discard transparent tail skeleton from squid body. Holding fins and squid body under cold running water, peel away reddish membrane. Similarly, peel off as much of the membranes on the tentacles as possible. Invert squid body and rinse it thoroughly.

Cut fins off squid and chop finely with the tentacles. Reserve. Set aside squid bodies.

Sauté onion, garlic and mushrooms in oil 5 minutes, stirring to coat well.

Raise heat, add chopped fins and tentacles, cook and stir 3 minutes. Remove from heat, add parsley, bread crumbs, cheese and seasonings. Adjust to taste and add more olive oil if too dry.

Stuff squid bodies, leaving 3/4-inch unfilled at end; skewer shut with a toothpick. If done ahead, chill until ready to use.

Sauté vegetables, garlic and parsley in oil 5 minutes; push to one side, raise heat and quickly brown squid on both sides. Remove squid and set aside.

Add tomatoes and anchovy paste; blend thoroughly.

Raise heat, add wine and boil rapidly 5 minutes. Add stocks, bring to boil, and add squid and fish. Cover and cook over medium heat 8 minutes; do not overcook or both the squid and the fish will toughen.

Adjust seasonings with salt, pepper and Tabasco.
Serves 6

Some Like it Cold

Many people, disenchanted with mere flavoring, sugar, cyclamates, saccharin, malt, hops, alcohol, fizz water, and other nonfoods, are discovering the pleasures of tasty cold soups served on the patio as well as in the dining room.

Here you'll find soups that are best cold, along with some equally good hot or cold. Elsewhere other soups, too, suggest serving cold as an option.

Dishes and soup should both be chilled in the refrigerator all day or overnight, and chilled individual bowls or serving bowl should be nested in crushed ice if at all possible. Adjust seasonings *after chilling*, embellish with any of the garnishes that appeal, and serve with toasts, croutons or other accompaniments.

VICHYSOISSE

6 thin leeks, white and some green, shredded
4 tablespoons finely chopped onion
1 garlic clove, finely chopped
4 tablespoons butter and/or rendered chicken fat

1-1/4 pints chicken stock, or combination of
  chicken and beef
1/8 teaspoon nutmeg or mace
1/4 teaspoon white pepper
3/4 pound floury potatoes, peeled and diced

1-1/4 pints milk
scant 1/2 pint double cream

salt
pepper
grated lemon peel

finely chopped fresh dill or spring onion tops

Sauté leeks, onion and garlic in butter and/or fat
until soft.
Add stock, seasonings and potatoes; cover, bring to
boil and simmer until potatoes are soft.
Purée in blender, add milk and cream, blend well
and chill.
Adjust seasonings to taste with salt, pepper and
grated lemon rind. Serve with a sprinkling of finely
chopped dill or spring onion tops.
Serves 6 - 8

CUCUMBER VICHYSOISSE

3 tablespoons finely chopped spring onions and tops
3 tablespoons finely chopped onion
1 tablespoon finely chopped shallots
6 - 8 tablespoons finely chopped celery
1 bunch (about 2 ounces) parsley, finely chopped
2 tablespoons butter

1-1/4 pints chicken stock
1 pound potatoes, peeled and diced
4 tablespoons finely chopped watercress
1/2 teaspoon thyme

3/4 pint sour cream
1/4 teaspoon salt
2 drops Tabasco

1 large cucumber, peeled, seeded and
  coarsely grated

creamy milk

paprika
finely chopped chives

Sauté spring onions, onion, shallots, celery and
parsley in butter until vegetables are soft but not
brown.
Add stock, potatoes, watercress and thyme. Cover,
bring to boil and simmer until potatoes are soft.
Purée in blender, cool and blend in sour cream,
seasonings and cucumber. Chill.
Adjust seasonings to taste; thin with creamy milk if
needed. Sprinkle with paprika and chopped chives.
Serves 6 - 8
Or garnish with extra watercress.

LOBSTER BISQUE

3 tablespoons chopped onion
2 tablespoons finely chopped celery
1 tablespoon finely chopped shallot
2 tablespoons butter
2 tablespoons flour

1/4 pint single cream
1/4 pint milk
1/2 pint chicken stock
4 tablespoons dry white wine

1 tablespoon butter
1 8-ounce lobster tail, cooked, shelled and
  finely chopped
4 tablespoons heated brandy

1/2 teaspoon salt
1/4 teaspoon white pepper
3 drops Tabasco

milk

paprika
finely chopped chives

Sauté onion, celery and shallots in butter 5 minutes, sprinkle with flour, cook and stir 3 minutes. Gradually add cream, milk, stock and wine; cook and stir until smooth and slightly thickened.
Melt butter. When bubbly, add lobster and cook rapidly, stirring, until heated through. Pour brandy over, ignite and let burn down.
Combine lobster and juices with cream sauce, cover and simmer 10 minutes. Purée in blender or sieve. Thin to desired consistency with milk, chill, adjust seasonings to taste, and serve with a sprinkling of paprika and finely chopped chives.
Serves 3 - 4

CURRIED CRAB OR LOBSTER SOUP

3 large tomatoes, chopped
6 - 8 tablespoons chopped onion
4 tablespoons chopped celery
2 tablespoons finely chopped green pepper
4 tablespoons finely chopped parsley
1 garlic clove, finely chopped
1 bay leaf
1/2 teaspoon basil
1/4 teaspoon tarragon
4 tablespoons raw long-grain rice
2 tablespoons butter
1/2 pint chicken stock
1/2 pint fish stock
1/4 pint single cream
1/4 pint milk
1/2 pound cooked crab or lobster, shredded

1 - 2 teaspoons curry powder
1/4 teaspoon white pepper

crab or diced lobster meat
finely chopped chives

Cook tomatoes, vegetables, parsley, garlic, herbs and rice in butter, covered, 10 minutes.
Add chicken stock and cook 30 minutes. Remove bay leaf and sieve.
Combine purée with fish stock, cream, milk and crab or lobster. Heat and add curry and pepper.
Chill, adjust seasonings with salt, and garnish with crab or diced lobster meat. Sprinkle with lots of finely chopped chives.
Serves 4 - 6

AVOCADO SOUP WITH PINEAPPLE

1 large ripe avocado
1-1/2 tablespoons lemon juice
6 - 8 tablespoons crushed canned pineapple, drained
1/2 pint rich chicken stock
1/8 teaspoon compound chili powder
1/4 teaspoon salt
1/8 teaspoon white pepper

garlic croutons
finely chopped fresh herbs (parsley, chervil,
   summer savory)
freshly ground pepper

Purée all ingredients except croutons, herbs and ground pepper in blender. Chill and adjust seasonings to taste. Serve with garlic croutons and a sprinkling of finely chopped fresh herbs.
Pass the peppermill.
Serves 3
Or serve with extra avocado brushed with lemon juice.

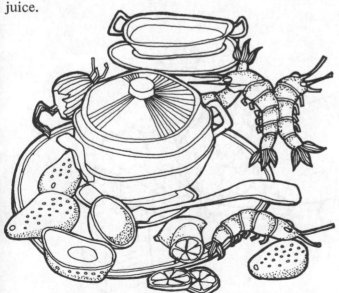

AVOCADO PURÉE

4 large ripe avocados
2 tablespoons lemon juice
1/4 pint sour cream
2 - 3 chicken stock cubes
3/4 pint milk
1/2 pint double cream
1/2 teaspoon salt
1/4 teaspoon white pepper
1/4 teaspoon garlic powder (optional)
1/4 teaspoon onion powder or
1 teaspoon grated onion

for garnish
fresh or canned prawns
finely chopped chervil
paprika
freshly ground pepper

Purée ingredients in blender and chill. Adjust seasonings to taste. Serve garnished with fresh or canned prawns, chopped chervil and a sprinkling of paprika.
Pass the peppermill.
Serves 4 - 6
Or flavor with white rum and/or curry; or sprinkle with lots of finely chopped fresh dill.

COLD ARTICHOKE PURÉE

1 14-ounce can water-pack artichoke hearts*
3/4 pint slightly gelatinous chicken stock
1/4 - 1/2 teaspoon oregano
1/2 teaspoon each salt and crumbled chicken
  stock cube
2 tablespoons lemon juice
1/4 pint creamy milk
1/4 pint double cream
thinly sliced lemon
finely chopped parsley and/or chives
sour cream whipped with soy sauce

*If using artichoke hearts canned in brine, rinse
  them thoroughly and use less salt in the seasoning
  if necessary.

*One hot, sunny day a confirmed soup-hater friend
accepted a cold cup of this soup with a glassy stare,
only to break into a puzzled smile as its refreshing
coolness and flavor took effect. Ever since, he's
been raving about it, and I think I have another
soup convert.*

Drain artichoke hearts and purée in blender with
stock and oregano. Pour into saucepan and heat
slowly. Season, add milk and cream, and adjust to
taste. Cool, chill and adjust seasoning.
Serve with garnish of thinly sliced lemon, finely
chopped parsley and/or chives and small dollops of
sour cream whipped with a little soy sauce.
Serves 3
Pass a tray of crab, fresh or canned prawns, and/or
julienne strips of cooked chicken or pork; tiny,
halved tomatoes; and melba toast.

PARSLEY VELOUTÉ

2 bunches parsley, tough stalks removed,
  finely chopped (8 - 10 ounces)
4 tablespoons finely chopped onion
2 tablespoons butter and/or rendered chicken fat
1 tablespoon flour
1-1/2 pints rich chicken stock

white pepper
cayenne
celery salt
lemon juice

2 egg yolks, beaten
1 pint creamy milk
about 1/2 pint double cream
salt

sour cream
tiny tomatoes, halved

Reserve 6 to 8 tablespoons parsley for garnish. Sauté rest of parsley and onion in butter and/or fat 5 minutes, stirring to coat. Sprinkle with flour, cook and stir 3 minutes, and gradually add stock. Cook and stir until smooth and slightly thickened. Cover and simmer gently 20 minutes. Purée in blender. Season with white pepper, cayenne, celery salt and lemon juice. Beat egg yolks and milk, whisk in 1/4 pint hot soup and return to rest of soup. Reheat but do not boil. Cool, chill thoroughly and thin with double cream if desired. Adjust seasonings with salt. Serve with dollops of sour cream, reserved parsley and halved tomatoes.
Serves 6 - 8
Or top with finely chopped raw mushrooms which have been sprinkled with lemon juice, and sprinkle with a little grated lemon rind.

FRESH GREEN BEAN PURÉE

1 pound green beans, cut up
3/4 pint each lamb and pork stock

1/4 pint sour cream
1/4 pint double cream
1/2 pint milk
1 teaspoon lemon juice

1/2 teaspoon salt
1/4 teaspoon white pepper
1/8 teaspoon summer savory

lemon slices
finely chopped parsley

The lamb and pork stock give the extra flavor!

Cook beans in stock until tender; purée in blender and cool.
Beat sour cream with a little double cream; combine with beans and season with lemon juice, salt, pepper and savory. Add remaining cream and milk.
Chill, adjust seasonings to taste and garnish with lemon slices and finely chopped parsley.
Serves 4 - 6

SORREL GAZPACHO

6 ounces sorrel, chopped
1-1/4 pints slightly gelatinous, rich chicken stock
1/2 chicken stock cube
1 garlic clove, finely chopped
1 hard-boiled egg, sliced
2 tablespoons lemon juice

1 well-beaten egg

salt, white pepper, paprika

1 large cucumber, peeled, halved, seeded and
  thinly sliced

peeled, seeded and diced tomato
thinly sliced onion
chopped chervil

Simmer sorrel in stock with stock cube, covered, 5 minutes. Remove from heat, add garlic and hard-boiled egg, and cool. Purée in blender and stir in lemon juice.
Pour mixture over beaten egg, beating thoroughly. Add salt, pepper and paprika to taste.
Stir in cucumber and refrigerate at least 4 hours. Serve with seeded, peeled and diced tomato, thinly sliced onion, and chopped chervil.
Serves 4
Or add thinly sliced courgettes, finely chopped spring onions, julienne strips of ham, and finely chopped dill and/or chives. May be served without puréeing.

FRESH ASPARAGUS PURÉE

2-1/2 pounds fresh asparagus, trimmed and washed
1 can (14-ounce) peeled tomatoes
1 teaspoon basil
1/4 teaspoon white pepper
2-1/2 pints chicken stock
2 tablespoons flour
1/4 pint sour cream

salt
creamy milk

Cut off 20 2-inch tips of asparagus and cut rest into 1-inch pieces. Cook the asparagus and tips, tomatoes, basil and pepper in 3/4 pint of the stock, removing the tips when they are just tender-crisp.
Reserve the tips for garnish. Continue cooking mixture 20 minutes or until stems are tender; purée in blender.
Combine remaining stock, flour and sour cream with purée; cook and stir until smooth and slightly thickened. Force through medium-fine sieve and add salt to taste. Thin with creamy milk if desired. Chill thoroughly, adjust seasoning and garnish with reserved asparagus tips. Serve with curried toast fingers (see page 181).
Serves 6 - 8
Or garnish with cooked crab and/or prawns, and a generous sprinkling of finely chopped parsley and chives.

GAZPACHO

3/4 pint gelatinous chicken stock
1-1/4 pints water
3 chicken stock cubes
1 large mild onion, thinly sliced
4 garlic cloves
4 - 8 tablespoons finely chopped green pepper

3 large tomatoes, peeled, seeded and very
  finely chopped
2 tablespoons very finely chopped green pepper
2 cucumbers, peeled, seeded and very finely chopped
1 clove garlic, *very* finely chopped
4 tablespoons very finely chopped celery
2 tablespoons very finely chopped mild onion
1-1/2 tablespoons lemon or lime juice
3 tablespoons olive oil
2 - 3 drops Tabasco and/or
1/4 teaspoon cumin

2 ripe avocados, peeled and cut in rings
2 cups herb croutons
extra finely chopped vegetables
finely chopped chives and parsley

This version of Gazpacho is very mild in comparison to many Spanish recipes. Increase the Tabasco, cumin and garlic for a spicier flavor.

Bring stock, water, stock cubes, onion, garlic and green pepper to a boil, simmer gently for 10 minutes, cool, strain and chill.

Gently stir in tomatoes, green pepper, cucumbers, garlic, celery, onion, lemon juice, olive oil, and Tabasco and/or cumin. Chill thoroughly and adjust seasoning to taste.

Serve in large chilled bowls, with an ice cube if desired, and garnish with avocado rings and herb croutons. Serve with extra chopped vegetables, chives and parsley.

Serves 6

Or add cooked rice or stale French bread cubes that have been soaked in garlic-flavored tomato juice, and diced, cooked prawns. Flavor with white-wine vinegar to taste.

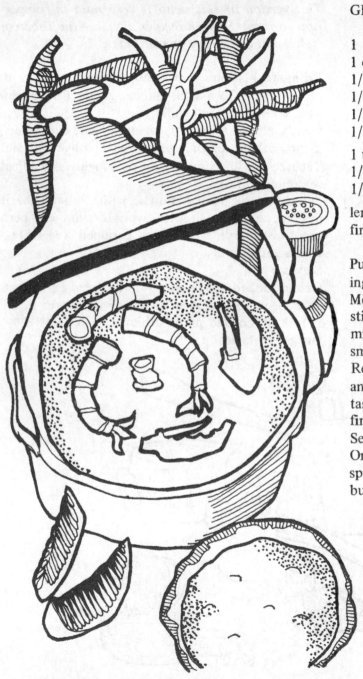

GREEN BEAN PURÉE

1 1-pound can green beans
1 chicken stock cube
1/2 teaspoon paprika
1/4 teaspoon tarragon
1/4 teaspoon basil
1/8 teaspoon white pepper

1 tablespoon each butter and flour
1/4 pint creamy milk
1/4 pint each double cream and sour cream

lemon or lime slices
finely chopped spring onion tops

Purée beans and their liquid, stock cube and seasonings in blender.
Melt butter until bubbly, sprinkle with flour, and stir and cook 3 minutes. Mix bean purée and creamy milk; gradually add to roux. Stir and cook until smooth and slightly thickened.
Return to blender and combine with double cream and sour cream. Cool, chill and adjust seasonings to taste. Serve with lemon or lime slices and lots of finely chopped spring onion tops.
Serves 3
Or garnish with fresh or canned prawns and/or crab, sprinkle with a little savory, and serve with buttered, toasted muffins.

DILLED SOUR CREAM SOUP

5 medium potatoes, peeled and sliced
1-1/2 pints water
2 sprigs fresh dill, chopped
1/2 teaspoon lemon juice
1/2 teaspoon salt

1-1/4 pints potato water
3/4 pint sour cream, scalded (stir while heating;
  be careful not to scorch)
1-1/2 tablespoons cornflour mixed with
  3 tablespoons cold water
2 ounces finely chopped fresh dill, no stems
1/4 pint sour cream, scalded
2 egg yolks, beaten

salt
white pepper
nutmeg
fronds of fresh dill (stripped from stems)

Cook potatoes, covered, in seasoned water until soft. Drain, reserving 1-1/4 pints of potato water (use the potatoes later).
Stir 3/4 pint of scalded sour cream into the hot potato water, add cornflour mixture and dill. Boil, stirring constantly, for 3 minutes.
Beat yolks into 1/4 pint scalded sour cream and combine with soup. Do not boil. Season, cool, chill, adjust seasoning and garnish with extra fronds of fresh dill.
Serves 4
Or sprinkle with a little grated lemon peel.

SPINACH PURÉE

1 pound fresh spinach, coarsely chopped
3/4 pint chicken stock
4 tablespoons chopped spring onions and tops
4 tablespoons finely chopped parsley
4 tablespoons finely chopped fresh dill

1/3 chicken stock cube
scant 1/2 pint water
pinch sugar
1/8 teaspoon nutmeg
1/2 teaspoon salt
1/4 teaspoon white pepper
8 fluid ounces double cream
2 tablespoons dry sherry

finely chopped hard-boiled egg
paprika
lemon wedges

Boil spinach in stock 10 minutes. Purée in blender with spring onions, parsley and dill.
Dissolve stock cube in water, blend with seasonings, spinach mixture, cream and sherry. Chill.
Adjust seasonings to taste. Sprinkle with chopped hard-boiled egg and paprika, and serve with lemon wedges.
Serves 4 - 6
Or float a teaspoon of peeled, seeded and coarsely grated cucumber on each portion of soup.

CUCUMBER MADRILENE

12 ounces cooked prawns
2 cucumbers, peeled, seeded and grated
4 tablespoons grated onion
2 teaspoons lemon juice
1/4 - 1/2 teaspoon salt
1/4 teaspoon white pepper
2 - 3 tablespoons finely chopped mint
1-1/4 pints consommé madrilene (see page 19)
finely chopped mint, to garnish

A most refreshing soup—easy to make and lovely to view.

Finely dice half of the prawns and combine with rest of ingredients. Chill until set. Serve with remaining prawns and more finely chopped mint.
Serves 6

CREAMY PUMPKIN SOUP

4 tablespoons finely chopped onion
2 tablespoons finely chopped leek, white and a
    little green
2 tablespoons butter

3/4 pint chicken stock
about 12 ounces fresh pumpkin, puréed after cooking in a little stock

1/2 teaspoon sugar
1/4 - 1/2 teaspoon mace
crumbled chicken stock cube
white pepper
salt
creamy milk

whipped cream

Sauté onion and leek in butter until soft. Add chicken stock and pumpkin; mix well and heat. Purée in blender and force through sieve.
Add seasonings, chill thoroughly and adjust seasonings to taste. Thin with milk if desired and serve with dollops of whipped cream.
Serves 4 - 6
Or garnish with coriander sprigs.

Hot or Cold

WATERCRESS SOUP

2 tablespoons finely chopped onion
2 teaspoons butter
about 4 ounces watercress, chopped
1-1/2 teaspoons flour
small piece chicken stock cube
1/4 teaspoon white pepper
1/4 teaspoon garlic powder
1 egg
3/4 pint chicken or veal stock

1/4 pint creamy milk
1/4 pint double cream

salt

lemon slices
1 hard-boiled egg, sieved

Sauté onions in butter until soft. Purée in blender with watercress, flour, stock cube, pepper, garlic powder, egg and half of the stock.
Combine with rest of stock and creamy milk. Cook in double boiler or heavy saucepan 30 minutes, stirring occasionally. Add double cream.
Chill, adjust seasonings with salt and garnish with lemon slices and hard-boiled egg.
Serves 2 - 4
To serve hot, reheat without boiling, adjust seasonings with salt and garnish with lemon slices and watercress sprigs.

COURGETTE PUREE

1-1/2 pounds courgettes, diced
6 - 8 tablespoons diced onion
1/2 teaspoon sugar
1/4 teaspoon salt
1/4 teaspoon oregano
2 sprigs chervil
1/2 pint chicken stock

1 tablespoon butter
1 tablespoon flour
1/2 pint milk
1/4 pint stock from courgettes

8 fluid ounces double cream

salt
white pepper

cooked crab meat
lemon slices
chervil sprigs

Cook courgettes, onion, seasonings and herbs in stock until vegetables are tender. Strain, reserving the liquid, and purée vegetables in blender.

Melt butter until bubbly, add flour and cook and stir 3 minutes. Gradually add milk and 1/4 pint reserved stock; cook and stir until smooth and slightly thickened. Add purée, blend well and stir in double cream.

Cool, chill, adjust seasonings with salt and pepper and garnish with crabmeat, sliced lemon and chervil sprigs.

Serves 4

To serve hot, thicken with 5 ounces fresh peas, cooked and puréed; substitute single cream for the double cream, and heat without boiling. Serve with lemon slices and garlic croutons.

CREAMY VEGETABLE MARROW SOUP

1 pound peeled, seeded and diced young
  vegetable marrow (prepared weight)
1 large onion, diced
1 stalk celery, diced
2 tablespoons chopped carrot
1 teaspoon basil
2 tablespoons butter

1 pint chicken stock

1/2 pint creamy milk
1/4 pint double cream

1/4 teaspoon sugar
1/8 teaspoon powdered cloves
1/8 teaspoon mace
1/4 teaspoon white pepper
1/2 teaspoon salt

paprika
finely chopped chives

Cook and stir vegetables and basil in butter 10 minutes.
Add stock, cover, bring to boil and simmer until vegetables are tender.
Purée in blender, add milk and cream, and heat with seasonings; do not boil.
Cool, chill and adjust seasonings.
Sprinkle with paprika and chives.
Serves 4 - 6
To serve hot, heat with a chiffonade of sorrel, spinach and lettuce (see page 179).

POTATO CELERIAC SOUP

5 - 6 ounces each diced celeriac and potato
6 - 8 tablespoons finely chopped onion
4 tablespoons finely chopped celery
2 tablespoons finely chopped leek
2 tablespoons finely chopped parsley
2 tablespoons butter

1-1/2 pints chicken or veal stock
1/4 teaspoon black pepper
2 bay leaves

2 egg yolks, beaten
1/2 pint creamy milk

1/4 pint double cream

salt

drained, finely chopped capers

Sauté vegetables and parsley in butter, stirring to coat well, 5 minutes.
Add stock, pepper and bay leaves. Cover, bring to boil and simmer until vegetables are soft. Discard bay leaves and purée vegetable mixture in blender. Reheat.
Beat egg yolks and creamy milk, whisk in 1/4 pint hot soup and return to rest of soup. Cool, add double cream and chill.
Adjust seasonings with salt and serve with capers.
Serves 4 - 6
To serve hot, omit double cream and increase the milk (or milk and single cream) to about 3/4 pint.
Garnish with finely chopped celery leaves.

CUCUMBER PURÉE

3 large cucumbers, peeled, seeded and diced
1 large onion, diced
3 tablespoons butter

2-1/2 tablespoons flour
1/2 teaspoon paprika
1/4 teaspoon each white pepper and celery salt
1/4 teaspoon basil or thyme
2 pints rich chicken stock
1/2 tablespoon lemon juice
2 tablespoons dry sherry or dry white wine
8 fluid ounces double cream

6 lemon slices
6 - 8 tablespoons peeled, seeded and finely chopped
    cucumber
2 tablespoons finely chopped fresh dill

Sauté cucumbers and onion in butter until slightly browned.
Sprinkle with flour, cook and stir 3 minutes, add seasonings, and gradually add 3/4 pint of the stock.
Cook and stir until smooth and slightly thickened. Cover and simmer 20 minutes.
Purée in blender, add remaining stock, reheat to blend, cool, and add lemon juice, sherry or wine, and cream. Chill and adjust seasonings to taste with salt, lemon juice and wine. Garnish with lemon slices, cucumber and dill.
Serves 6
To serve hot, substitute creamy milk (or milk and single cream) for the double cream, and heat without boiling. Adjust seasonings and garnish with sour cream beaten with a little soy sauce, lemon slices and very finely chopped green pepper.

CARROT CRÈME

1-1/2 pounds carrots, sliced
2 tablespoons chopped onion
1/2 teaspoon each sugar and marjoram
1/4 teaspoon thyme
2 tablespoons butter

2 tablespoons flour
3/4 pint milk
1 bay leaf
1 chicken stock cube
1/2 pint milk
1/2 pint single cream

salt

finely chopped mint

Steam carrots, onion and seasonings in butter, covered, until carrots are tender.
Sprinkle with flour, cook and stir until browned slightly, and gradually add milk, stirring until smooth. Add bay leaf, cover and simmer gently 30 minutes, stirring occasionally.
Discard bay leaf and purée soup in blender. Add chicken stock cube, milk and cream, and reheat without boiling.
Chill, adjust seasonings to taste and sprinkle with finely chopped mint.
Serves 4 - 6
Serve hot garnished with plenty of grated raw carrot and finely chopped chervil.

CREAM OF TOMATO SOUP

1 can (14-ounce) peeled tomatoes, chopped
6 - 8 tablespoons chopped celery
4 tablespoons each chopped carrot and onion
1 teaspoon sugar
1/2 teaspoon basil
1 parsley sprig
1 marjoram sprig
1 bay leaf
1 tablespoon unsalted butter
1/4 pint chicken stock
1 chicken stock cube

2 tablespoons butter
2 tablespoons flour
1/4 pint double cream
1/2 pint milk

1/4 teaspoon paprika
1/4 teaspoon white pepper

4 tablespoons sour cream
salt
basil
peeled, seeded and diced tomato, or
4 tablespoons mayonnaise flavored to taste
  with curry powder
2 tablespoons finely chopped parsley

Simmer tomatoes, celery, carrot, onion, sugar, herbs and butter in stock with stock cube until vegetables are soft. Discard marjoram sprig and bay leaf; force vegetables through food mill.

Melt butter until bubbly, add flour, cook and stir 3 minutes. Gradually add cream and milk; cook and stir until smooth and slightly thickened.

Add vegetable purée, paprika and pepper; simmer, stirring occasionally, 20 minutes.

Blend in sour cream and heat just to melt; do not boil. Cool, chill and adjust seasonings with salt and basil. Garnish with peeled, seeded and diced tomato, or dollops of curry-flavored mayonnaise and finely chopped parsley.

Serves 6

To serve hot simply heat without boiling, adjust seasonings and garnish with finely chopped artichoke hearts and a sprinkling of finely chopped fresh basil.

Fruit Soups

Only the pure in heart can make a good soup
—Beethoven, 1824

Fruit soups are especially popular in Germany as desserts and in the Scandinavian countries for breakfast and lunch. Fruit soups should all be icy cold and served in chilled bowls. Combinations of fresh and dried fruits offer varying degrees of sweetness and tartness. I've found that if a fruit soup is too syrupy or tart it's better to add light wine than more water. A dash of liqueur with its own bite can add an interesting contrast, too.

SCANDINAVIAN FRUIT SOUP

12 ounces mixed dried fruits
6 - 8 tablespoons golden seedless raisins
2 tablespoons dried currants
2 pints water

1 orange, sliced 1/4-inch thick
1 lemon, sliced 1/4-inch thick
6 - 8 tablespoons each currant jelly and sugar
2 tablespoons quick-cooking tapioca
1/4 teaspoon salt
1 pint unsweetened pineapple juice
1 large eating apple, peeled, cored and
  diced (optional)

An especially attractive soup—marvelous for brunch!

Combine fruits, raisins, currants and water. Cover, bring to boil and cook until tender.
Add remaining ingredients and simmer 10 minutes.
Cool, chill and serve with crisp French rolls and unsalted butter.
Serves 8 - 10
Or add about 1/4 pint port.

PLUM SOUP

1 pound plums, stoned and chopped
4 tablespoons crumbled rusks
6 - 8 tablespoons each dry white wine and apple juice
small pinch cinnamon, cloves and ginger

2 tablespoons double cream
1 teaspoon sugar
1/2 teaspoon lemon juice
4 tablespoons Rhine wine

apple slices brushed with lemon juice

Cook plums, rusk crumbs, wine, apple juice and spices until plums are soft. Sieve.
Add cream, sugar, lemon juice, and wine. Chill and adjust seasonings to taste, adding more chilled wine if desired.
Garnish with thin slices of unpeeled apple brushed with lemon juice to prevent discoloring.
Serves 3 - 4

ICY WATERMELON SOUP

1/2 medium watermelon
about 1/2 pint Rhine wine

5 ounces sugar
generous 1/4 pint water
4 slices lemon or lime
1 2-inch piece vanilla pod

very finely chopped mint

Scoop 12 balls from seedless portion of water-melon. Combine with wine and chill.
Simmer sugar, water, lemon or lime slices and vanilla pod, covered, 20 minutes. Discard lemon slices and vanilla pod.
Put 3/4 pound watermelon cubes, seeds removed, in blender; pour in sugar syrup and blend until smooth.
Chill, combine with melon balls and wine, and adjust to taste.
Sprinkle with very finely chopped mint.
Serves 6

CANTALOUPE SOUP

1 large cantaloupe melon
5 tablespoons butter
2 teaspoons sugar
1 teaspoon freshly grated lemon rind
1/16 teaspoon powdered ginger
pinch salt

1 pint milk

white rum and/or lemon juice

sprigs of mint

Scoop out a cup of melon balls and reserve for garnish. Scrape out seeds and dice remaining flesh.

Sauté diced melon in butter with sugar, lemon rind, ginger and salt until soft.
Add milk, bring to boil and simmer 10 minutes.
Purée in blender, cool and chill. Adjust seasonings with lemon juice and/or rum.
Garnish with reserved cantaloupe and sprigs of mint.
Serves 4

RASPBERRY SOUP

10 - 12 ounces frozen raspberries, thawed
1 11-ounce can mandarin oranges and juice
1/4 pint orange juice
4 tablespoons dry red wine
3 - 4 tablespoons castor sugar
4 tablespoons lemon juice
1/2 pint dry white wine
1 tablespoon kirsch

very finely chopped mint
mint sprigs

Pretty and refreshing!

Combine ingredients and chill.
Adjust to taste with additional sugar, lemon juice and/or wine or kirsch.
Sprinkle with very finely chopped mint and garnish with mint sprigs.
Serves 6

GARLIC AND FRUIT SOUP

3 - 5 garlic cloves, finely chopped
5 tablespoons slivered blanched almonds
3 slices white bread, crusts removed, diced
2-1/2 tablespoons olive oil
1-1/2 pints chicken or veal stock
1/2 teaspoon salt
1/4 teaspoon white pepper
2 tablespoons dry white wine

3 ounces cantaloupe balls, chilled
1 bunch seedless white grapes, chilled
4 ounces raw prosciutto or Westphalian ham sliced
    paper thin and torn into strips

toasted, blanched, slivered almonds

Purée garlic and almonds in blender and sauté
with bread in oil until golden.
Add stock, salt and pepper and cook 10 minutes.
Return to blender and purée. Cool.
Add wine, chill and adjust seasonings to taste.
Garnish with melon balls, grapes and ham, serve
with a dish of toasted, blanched slivered almonds.
Serves 4 - 6

STRAWBERRY-WINE SOUP

12 ounces fresh strawberries, sliced
6 tablespoons sugar
scant 1/2 pint water

2 teaspoons cornflour mixed with
1 tablespoon cold water

1/2 pint dry white wine
1 - 2 tablespoons lemon juice
2 teaspoons grated lemon peel

brandy

lemon peel strips

Combine strawberries, sugar and water; simmer
until berries are soft.
Stir in cornflour mixture, and cook and stir until
thickened. Purée in blender.
Add wine, lemon juice and lemon peel. Chill and
flavor to taste with lemon juice, wine, brandy and
more sugar if necessary.
Garnish with tiny lemon peel strips.
Serves 4

Or can also purée with 4 tablespoons sour cream.

BLACK CHERRY SOUP

1 pound fresh black cherries, pitted and chopped
6 tablespoons orange juice
1-1/2 tablespoons lemon juice
4 tablespoons dry sherry

Rhine wine, well chilled

orange and lemon slices

Purée 1/2 cup cherries with the orange juice in blender. Combine with lemon juice and sherry. Add remainder of chopped cherries.
Chill, add wine to taste and adjust, adding sugar if needed.
Float thin slices of orange and lemon on top.
Serves 4

TOMATO-ORANGE SOUP

3/4 pint each tomato and orange juice
2 tablespoons lemon juice
6 - 8 tablespoons dry white wine
1/4 teaspoon finely chopped fresh basil
salt
cayenne pepper
black pepper

whipped cream
finely chopped chives

Combine juices, wine and basil. Chill, adjust with salt, cayenne and pepper. Garnish with dollops of whipped cream and finely chopped chives.
Serves 4 - 6

BRANDIED PEACH & PLUM SOUP

1 pound each fresh peaches and plums,
  stoned and diced
generous 1/2 pint each water and dry red wine
5 ounces sugar
1 slice lemon
1 4-inch cinnamon stick

2 tablespoons brandy

very finely chopped mint

Cook peaches, plums, water, wine, sugar, lemon and cinnamon, covered, until fruits are soft. Discard lemon and cinnamon; force fruits through sieve.
Add brandy, chill and adjust to taste, adding sugar and/or brandy as needed.
Garnish with very finely chopped mint.
Serves 6

MIXED FRUIT SOUP

2 pounds fresh fruit (plums, apricots, cherries,
  apples, peaches), pitted and diced
1-1/4 pints water
3 tablespoons sugar
2 slices lemon
1 4-inch cinnamon stick
2 tablespoons raspberry juice

4 tablespoons orange juice
2 teaspoons lemon juice

6 tablespoons port
sugar

sour cream
mint sprigs

Cook fruit, water, sugar, lemon slices and cinnamon, covered, until fruit is soft. Discard lemon and cinnamon; force fruit through sieve.
Add juices and port; chill and adjust to taste with juice, sugar and/or port.
Serve with dollops of well-beaten sour cream and garnish with mint sprigs.
Serves 6

MORELLO CHERRY SOUP

1 pint water
6 ounces castor sugar
1 3-inch cinnamon stick
2 pounds morello cherries, pitted

1 tablespoon cornflour
2 tablespoons water
4 tablespoons each dry red wine and double
 cream

Cherry Heering to taste (about 1/4 pint)

mint

Bring water, sugar, cinnamon and cherries to boil. Simmer 30 minutes. Blend cornflour and water, stir into cherries and cook and stir until clear and slightly thickened. Remove about a cup of cherries and some juice; purée in blender and return to rest of soup. Cool, add wine and cream, blend and chill thoroughly.
Just before serving add chilled Cherry Heering to taste; serve in chilled bowls garnished with mint.
Serves 6 - 8
Or serve with dollops of sour cream.

APFELSUPPE

4 large tart apples, cored and diced
4 slices lemon
1 1-inch cinnamon stick
1 pint water

1/4 pint sour cream, beaten (at room temperature)
3 - 4 tablespoons castor sugar

generous 1/2 pint claret or rosé wine
1-2 teaspoons lemon juice

cinnamon
mint sprigs

Cook apples, lemon and cinnamon in water until apples are soft.
Remove lemon and cinnamon stick, and sieve apples, forcing as much pulp through as possible.
Beat 1/4 pint apple mixture with sour cream and return to rest of soup. Add sugar and blend well.
Gradually stir in wine, add lemon juice and chill. Adjust with more sugar, wine and/or lemon juice.
Sprinkle with a little cinnamon and serve with a garnish of mint sprigs.
Serves 4 - 6

RHUBARB FRUIT SOUP

6 ounces castor sugar
1-1/2 pints water
1 3-inch cinnamon stick
6 ounces dried apricots, cut in quarters
1 pound rhubarb, diced

2 tablespoons cornflour
3 tablespoons cold water
8-10 ounces frozen raspberries, thawed and drained
1 tablespoon lemon juice

grated orange rind
sliced strawberries

Combine sugar, water, cinnamon and apricots. Bring to boil, cover and simmer 5 minutes. Add rhubarb, bring back to boil and simmer until rhubarb is barely tender.
Mix cornflour and water (or use juice from drained raspberries) and add to fruit; cook and stir until slightly thickened and clear. Add raspberries and lemon juice; adjust sugar to taste. Chill.
Garnish with grated orange rind and strawberries.
Serves 6 - 8

APRICOT WINE SOUP

1/4 pound dried apricots
1 small tart eating apple, peeled, cored and diced
1/2 pint water

1/2 pint apricot nectar
1/2 pint apple juice
4 tablespoons orange juice
1/4 pint sour cream

generous 1/4 pint chilled dry white wine

mint sprigs

Cook apricots and apple in water, covered, until apricots are soft, adding more water if needed.
Purée in blender with nectar, apple juice, orange juice and sour cream.
Chill, add wine to taste, and serve with sprigs of mint.
Serves 6 - 8

Mini Recipes

Though I feel a cook can make the best soups and derive the most satisfaction by starting from scratch, I'm not a purist in this matter.

There is no reason why one shouldn't take advantage of factory-prepared foods when time is short or the larder is low. There are many ways of adding a personal touch, however, and of making a good commercial product into something even better. Check the garnitures (page 180) for other ideas, and endless combinations.

1. Substitute 1/2 can rosé wine for part of the water to be mixed with a can of condensed cream of chicken soup. Garnish with lime or lemon slices.

2. Combine and heat 1 can each condensed cream of mushroom soup and asparagus soup (or tomato and pea), 1-1/2 cans milk, 1/2 can single cream and 8 ounces flaked crabmeat. Just before serving, add 4 tablespoons dry sherry and 2 tablespoons (1 ounce) finely diced butter.

3. Combine and heat 3 cans condensed cream of celery soup, 2 cans milk, 1/2 can double cream, 8 ounces prawns, crab or lobster and 6 to 8 tablespoons shredded mild Cheddar cheese. Garnish with sliced black or stuffed green olives.

4. Simmer 3 cans condensed consommé and 1 can water with 12 parsley sprigs for 30 minutes. Remove parsley, chill until firm and break up with fork into chilled bowls. Serve with sour cream and black caviar or lumpfish roe.

5. Sauté 4 tablespoons finely chopped onion in 2 tablespoons butter until soft. Add and heat 2 cans condensed cream of vegetable soup, 1-1/2 cans milk and 8 ounces prawns, finely chopped. Add 4 ounces tomatoes, peeled and diced; reheat briefly and sprinkle with finely chopped dill.

6. Combine 1 can condensed consommé, 6 to 8 tablespoons diced prawns, 4 tablespoons finely chopped celery, 2 tablespoons chopped watercress, and black pepper to taste. Chill until firm, break up with fork and serve with lemon wedges and watercress.

7. Purée 1/2 soup can milk and 1 can chopped cooked broccoli in blender. Mix with 1 can condensed cream of mushroom, celery or chicken soup and 1 can milk. Heat and serve with lemon slices and garlic croutons.

8. Heat 1 can condensed consommé, 1/2 can water in which you have softened 1 teaspoon powdered gelatine, and 2 tablespoons sherry. Cool, chill until firm and serve with avocado rings.

9. Combine and heat 1 can each condensed cream of chicken and cream of celery soup and 2 cans milk. Cool, chill and garnish with chopped, peeled and seeded cucumber, fresh mint or chopped celery leaves.

10. Combine and heat 1 can each condensed cream of vegetable soup, pea soup and tomato soup, and 2 cans milk. Garnish with pimiento slivers.

11. Combine and heat 1 can condensed cream of mushroom soup, 1 can cream of chicken soup, 1 can water and a 12-ounce can whole kernel corn, and dry sherry. Sprinkle with crumbled crisp-fried bacon and finely chopped parsley.

12. Combine and heat 1 can condensed cream of mushroom soup, 1 can creamy corn and 1-1/2

cans milk. Garnish with slivers of raw sweet red pepper.

13. Combine and heat 1 can each condensed cream of celery soup and cream of tomato soup, and 1-1/2 cans milk. Serve with sliced cooked frankfurters.

14. Combine and heat 1 can each condensed cream of mushroom soup and chicken soup, 1 can condensed consommé and 1-1/2 cans evaporated milk. Rub through sieve and season with curry powder to taste. Serve hot or cold, sprinkled with finely chopped chives.

15. Combine 2 cans condensed consommé, 6 ounces prawns, finely chopped, 4 tablespoons thinly sliced celery, 2 tablespoons each finely chopped parsley and watercress, and 1/8 teaspoon white pepper. Chill and garnish with lime or lemon wedges, extra whole prawns and parsley.

16. Purée 1 can each condensed cream of mushroom soup and cream of chicken soup, 1 small can mushrooms, drained, 1-1/4 pounds frozen chopped spinach, defrosted, 2 teaspoons onion flakes and 1/4 teaspoon finely chopped garlic. Combine and heat with 1 pint milk and salt and pepper to taste. Garnish with sliced hard-boiled eggs and paprika.

17. Combine 1 can condensed cream of tomato soup, 1 can milk, 1/4 pint double cream, 5 ounces creamy cottage cheese, 1/2 teaspoon

Worcestershire sauce, and Tabasco and salt to taste. Chill, adjust seasoning and serve in chilled bowls, garnished with slivered spring onions.

18. Purée 1 can condensed cream of celery soup, 1 can milk, 1/4 pint double cream, 4 ounces watercress leaves and some stems, and 1 medium-sized cucumber, peeled, seeded and chopped. Add salt to taste, chill, adjust seasoning and serve in chilled bowls, garnished with finely chopped watercress.

19. Purée 1 soup can tomato juice, 3 tablespoons each finely chopped parsley and onion, 1 large tomato, peeled and diced, 3 tablespoons sour cream and 1/2 can condensed consommé. Chill, stir and season to taste with Tabasco and Worcestershire sauce. Serve in chilled bowls.

20. Lace well-flavored home-made beef or chicken stock with dry sherry. Sprinkle with chives or shredded Cheddar cheese.

21. Bring 1/2 pint rich home-made beef stock, 3/4 pint tomato juice, 1 teaspoon Worcestershire sauce and 2 tablespoons lemon juice just to boil. Cool, chill and serve icy cold, garnished with julienne strips of pickled beetroot and shredded lobster or finely chopped prawns.

22. Sauté 1/2 pound sliced mushrooms, 6 to 8 tablespoons finely chopped onion and 6 parsley sprigs in 1 tablespoon butter until soft. Add 2 pints well-flavored chicken stock, cover, bring to boil

and simmer 40 minutes. Strain, reheat, add 4 tablespoons dry sherry and garnish with sautéed mushroom caps and lemon wedges.

23. Flavor rich home-made beef consommé with lemon juice and garnish with lemon slices. Add dry white wine just before serving.

24. Heat 2-1/2 pints well-flavored chicken stock, 1/4 teaspoon grated lime or lemon peel and 3 tablespoons lime or lemon juice. Garnish with lime or lemon slices.

25. Boil 6 to 8 tablespoons rice in 2 pints home-made chicken stock for 15 to 20 minutes. Beat 2 egg yolks with 1/4 pint double cream. Whisk in 1/4 pint hot soup and return to rest of soup. Reheat without boiling, stirring, and add 2 or 3 tablespoons port. Sprinkle with parsley.

26. Heat rich home-made beef consommé with chopped celery stalks and leaves for 30 minutes. Strain and serve with finely chopped celery and paprika.

27. Blend 3 eggs, 4 tablespoons dry sherry, 1/8 teaspoon nutmeg or mace and 2 tablespoons lemon or lime juice. Slowly pour in 1-1/4 pints well-flavored hot chicken stock and blend for 1 minute. Garnish with finely chopped chervil and diced artichoke hearts.

28. Serve jellied consommé (home-made or canned) with crumbled Roquefort cheese and finely chopped chives.

29. Purée 12 ounces peeled, seeded and diced cucumber, 3 spring onions, 2 tablespoons finely chopped parsley, 1 tablespoon finely chopped fresh dill, 3/4 pint buttermilk and 4 tablespoons sour cream. Chill. Season with salt and serve in chilled bowls. Pass the peppermill.

30. Heat equal amounts of canned clam juice and tomato juice. Garnish with lime or lemon slices.

31. Heat 3/4 pint vegetable juice, 1/4 pint pineapple juice, 1/2 teaspoon Worcestershire sauce and 3 drops Tabasco. Sprinkle with finely chopped chives or green pepper.

32. Purée in blender 3/4 pint chilled tomato juice, 1/2 teaspoon salt, 1/4 teaspoon each pepper and basil, 1/8 teaspoon marjoram and 5 tablespoons sour cream. Chill and garnish with finely chopped chives and lemon slices. Serve in chilled bowls.

33. Keep this blend in the refrigerator (or freezer) for a quick cold soup. Cook 1-1/2 pounds sliced carrots and 2 tablespoons raw rice in 1-1/2 pints stock until carrots are soft and rice is tender. Purée in blender and refrigerate. When ready to serve, thin to desired consistency with creamy milk. Season to taste with salt, pepper, Worcestershire sauce and Tabasco. Garnish with finely chopped chives or shredded raw carrot and parsley sprigs. Or thin with milk and sour cream.

Soup Garnishes

A soup is not the beautiful soup Alice in Wonderland extolls without a pretty serving bowl, attractive table or tray settings and appropriate individual dishes. Colorful and tasty trimmings of various shapes and sizes, some in the soup itself, others alongside on the plate, add pleasure to both the eye and the palate.

You may want to experiment with the more unusual suggestions that follow before actually serving them to guests.

Cook and try a dumpling or meatball first so you can adjust seasonings to your taste before cooking the entire batch.

POTATO DUMPLINGS

3 large potatoes, boiled soft and
  refrigerated overnight
4 tablespoons flour
1 egg, beaten fluffy
1/2 teaspoon salt
1/4 teaspoon nutmeg or oregano
1 tablespoon *very* finely chopped parsley

Grate the potatoes to make about 1-1/4 pounds.
Mix in flour, egg, seasonings and parsley, adding
a little more flour if needed to make a workable
dough.
Form into balls the size of large marbles and
cook in salted water kept at low boil until balls
rise to surface.
Makes about 25

EGG DUMPLINGS

6 hard-boiled egg yolks
1/2 teaspoon flour
2 eggs, beaten
1 teaspoon salt
1/4 teaspoon pepper
1/2 teaspoon curry or nutmeg

Mash yolks and flour and mix in raw eggs and
seasonings, adding more flour to make a workable
dough.
Form into small balls or drop by half-teaspoonfuls
into gently boiling salted water. Cook 5 minutes or
until balls rise to surface.
Makes about 25

BUTTER DUMPLINGS

1 egg, beaten
3-1/2 tablespoons softened butter
1/4 teaspoon salt
pinch finely grated lemon peel
dash celery salt
dash paprika
dash thyme
1 teaspoon very finely chopped parsley
1/2 teaspoon very finely chopped chives
5-1/2 tablespoons flour

Mix egg, butter and seasonings. Stir in flour and let
stand at room temperature 1 hour.
Drop by teaspoonfuls into gently boiling salted
water or broth. They will be cooked when they rise
to the top.
Makes about 20

EGG FOAM DUMPLINGS

1 egg white, beaten stiff

1 egg yolk, beaten
1/4 teaspoon salt
1/8 teaspoon white pepper
1/8 teaspoon grated nutmeg
1 tablespoon each grated Parmesan cheese and
  fine stale bread crumbs

Combine yolk, seasonings, cheese and bread
crumbs. Gently fold into egg white and drop by
tablespoonfuls into well-seasoned stock kept at
slow boil. Simmer 5 minutes.
Makes about 12

MARROW DUMPLINGS

2 3-inch beef marrow bones
1-1/2 tablespoons softened butter
1 egg
1 tablespoon finely chopped parsley
6 tablespoons stale fine bread crumbs
1/4 teaspoon each salt and baking powder
1/8 teaspoon each black pepper and nutmeg

Push marrow from bones to make 3 tablespoons, mash with fork and mix in butter. Combine with rest of ingredients and form into small balls the size of a nutmeg.
Drop into gently boiling water and cook about 5 minutes until balls are slightly puffed and rise to top.
Be careful not to overcook.
Makes about 20 — extra good in tomato soup.

BREAD DUMPLINGS

2 eggs, beaten
1-1/2 ounces fine bread crumbs
1/2 teaspoon cornflour
1 - 2 teaspoons milk
2 teaspoons very finely chopped parsley
1/2 teaspoon salt
1/8 teaspoon onion powder
1/8 teaspoon grated lemon peel

Mix ingredients thoroughly and chill at least 1 hour. Form into 24 small balls and cook in simmering salted water 3 minutes after balls rise to the surface and puff up.

ALMOND DUMPLINGS

5 ounces plain cracker crumbs, finely crushed
2-1/2 ounces blanched almonds, coarsely ground
6 - 8 tablespoons milk
1 beaten egg
3 tablespoons browned butter
1 teaspoon salt
1/8 teaspoon white pepper
1/8 teaspoon garlic powder
1/8 teaspoon grated lemon peel

flour

Mix ingredients, chill and form into small balls, using flour if needed to make a workable dough.
Drop into gently boiling salted water or stock; cook 5 minutes or until balls rise to surface.
Makes about 30

MATZO DUMPLINGS

8 tablespoons Matzo meal
8 tablespoons well-drained, cooked chopped spinach
or 8 tablespoons cooked minced pork, chicken, beef, liver, ham or turkey
or 4 tablespoons grated cheese or minced cooked bacon or combinations

Follow package directions for mixing Matzo balls. Use plain or add optional ingredients.
Follow package directions for cooking, but watch carefully — 20 minutes seems long enough.
Makes about 40

CHOUX DUMPLINGS

8 tablespoons water
2 tablespoons butter
6 tablespoons flour
1 egg
1 tablespoon finely chopped parsley
1/2 tablespoon finely chopped chives
1/4 teaspoon salt
1/2 teaspoon celery salt or
1/4 teaspoon dried dill and
generous pinch grated lemon peel
1 tablespoon lemon juice
dash nutmeg

Bring water to boil with butter to melt butter. Add flour and stir vigorously until dough leaves side of saucepan. Cool slightly, beat in egg and rest of ingredients, mixing thoroughly.
Drop by teaspoonfuls into gently boiling salted water or directly into broth. Simmer until balls rise to top.
Makes about 25

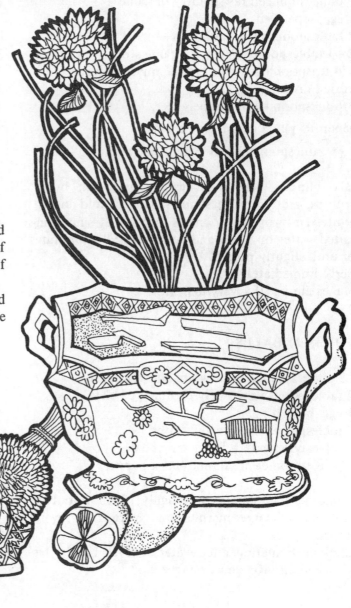

QUENELLES

8 ounces minced raw poultry or game
1 egg, separated
2 tablespoons breadcrumbs
2 - 3 tablespoons poultry or game stock
1/4 teaspoon each salt, thyme, onion powder and
  dried dill
1/8 teaspoon white pepper

generous pinch grated lemon peel

4 - 6 tablespoons lightly beaten egg white

Mix minced poultry or game, egg yolk, bread crumbs, stock and seasonings. Gently fold in egg white. Drop by teaspoonfuls into gently simmering salted water or broth and cook carefully 4 minutes or until slightly puffed.
Serve immediately.
Makes about 30 — very delicate!

CHICKEN BALLS

12 ounces minced raw white chicken meat
2 tablespoons very finely chopped parsley
1 egg, beaten
8 tablespoons fine bread crumbs
1 tablespoon grated Parmesan cheese
1/4 teaspoon each salt and black pepper

Combine ingredients thoroughly, form into balls the size of large marbles and refrigerate several hours.
Cook in simmering salted water or stock 10 minutes.
Makes about 40 — may be frozen

FORCEMEAT BALLS

2 hard-boiled egg yolks
1/4 pound minced cooked meat or poultry or game
1 teaspoon milk
3 tablespoons fine bread crumbs
1 beaten egg
1 teaspoon flour
1/4 teaspoon salt
1/8 teaspoon white pepper

Mash egg yolks with milk and mix with rest of ingredients. Flour hands and form small balls the size of a nutmeg. Drop into gently boiling water or broth and cook carefully until they rise to top.
Makes about 25
The broth should match the meat used in the balls.

KOENIGSBERGER KLOPPS

1/4 pound each minced beef and pork
2 ounces minced veal
4 tablespoons grated onion
1-1/2 tablespoons grated lemon peel
1 tablespoon lemon juice
2 slices white bread soaked in milk and
  squeezed dry
1 *small* egg
1/2 teaspoon salt
1/4 teaspoon black pepper

Combine ingredients thoroughly, form into balls the size of large marbles and refrigerate several hours.
Cook in simmering salted water or stock 10 minutes.
Makes about 40 — may be frozen

CHIFFONADE

Sauté 8 tablespoons finely shredded sorrel, spinach, lettuce or kale, or combinations in 2 tablespoons butter.

FONDUE TOPPING

Heat 8 tablespoons dry white wine in heavy pan or double boiler. Mix 8 tablespoons shredded Gruyère cheese and 1/2 teaspoon cornflour; gradually add to wine. Cook gently to melt and serve on hot soup.

AIOLI SAUCE

Purée 2 - 4 chopped garlic cloves, 1 egg yolk, 1/4 teaspoon salt and 1 teaspoon lemon juice in blender. Turn on high and in a steady stream add 1/4 pint olive oil. Adjust seasonings with salt and pepper.

ROYALES

Simmer 1/4 pint rich stock with 1 chopped garlic clove, 2 large sprigs parsley or chervil, and 1/8 teaspoon each savory and paprika for 10 minutes. Strain, cool and beat in 1 beaten egg and 1 beaten egg yolk. Sieve into buttered square baking dish or tin. Stand the dish in a larger pan with 1 inch hot water and bake 20 to 30 minutes in a 350°F/Mark 4/180°C oven until knife inserted in middle comes out clean. Cool, chill and cut into dice, or use small decorative cutters.
Or, after sieving, add 2 tablespoons of any minced cooked vegetable, meat, poultry, game, liver or bacon.

CREAM, GRILLED

Whip 1/4 pint double cream, add 2 tablespoons dry sherry, and spoon over soup in 6 ovenproof bowls. Set 6 inches below heat and grill 1 minute. Watch carefully! Or whip 4 tablespoons cream and combine with 4 tablespoons Hollandaise or mayonnaise.

CREPES

Mix 1 egg, 1/2 egg shell of milk, 1 tablespoon flour and 1/8 teaspoon salt; add finely chopped parsley or chives, if desired. Melt 1/8 teaspoon butter in 7-inch pancake pan, pour in half the batter, tip pan to coat bottom and brown. Turn and brown other side. Repeat with rest of batter. Roll, cut into strips, and garnish soup.

GARNITURES

Finely chopped herbs and spices: chives, dill, chervil, curly parsley, flat leaf parsley, coriander, rosemary, mint, fennel, spring onions, celery leaves, watercress, lovage, borage, ginger, toasted poppy or sesame seeds, chopped sorrel.

Blanched or browned vegetable dice or julienne strips: celeriac, beetroots, carrots, turnips, potatoes, artichoke hearts, asparagus tips, mild onions, celery, green or red peppers, green beans, leeks, mushrooms, spinach.

Uncooked vegetable dice or julienne strips: radishes, red or green peppers, carrots, celery, avocados, tomatoes, mushrooms, cucumbers.

Cooked poultry, game, meat dice or julienne strips

Citrus, sliced or wedged; grated peel, curls or tiny strips

Others: popcorn, slivered toasted almonds, chopped, sliced or sieved hard-boiled eggs, sour cream with soy or paprika or caviar, double cream whipped with soy or paprika, grated cheeses, cheese balls, pork or bacon cracklings, sausages, rice, pastas, shellfish, olives, capers, pickles.

CROUTONS

Dry in cool oven sliced white, pumpernickel, rye, or French bread cut into 1/2-inch squares. Toss 3 cups of croutons with 1/4 cup melted butter mixed with one of the following mixtures and brown in 300°F/Mark 2/150°C oven, turning often.

1) 4 tablespoons grated Parmesan, 1 teaspoon paprika, dash cayenne
2) 1/2 teaspoon salt, 1 to 2 teaspoons mixed dried herbs, pepper
3) 1-1/2 tablespoons lemon juice, 1 tablespoon grated lemon rind, 1 teaspoon paprika
4) 2 grated garlic cloves, 1/2 teaspoon oregano, salt, pepper
5) salt and cayenne pepper
6) 2 tablespoons grated Parmesan, 1 teaspoon paprika, 1/2 teaspoon garlic powder, 1/2 teaspoon onion juice

Bake in 275°F/Mark 1/140°C oven, turning often, 1/2 to 1 hour until crisp and golden.

Accompaniments

SESAME WAFERS

Sift 8 ounces plain flour with 1 teaspoon garlic powder and 1/2 teaspoon salt. Cut in 4 ounces butter until crumbly, stir in 6 to 8 tablespoons sour cream lightly, using a fork to mix until *just* blended, and form into ball. Wrap in greaseproof paper, chill several hours, roll 1/4-inch thick, cut into shapes and place on baking sheet. Brush with water and sprinkle with sesame seeds. Bake in 400°F/Mark 6/ 200°C oven 15 minutes or until slightly puffed and golden.

RYE CRISPS

Use slightly stale, thinly sliced continental rye bread: 1) spread with melted butter, sprinkle with salt and caraway seeds, bake in a very cool oven until crisp; 2) spread both sides with melted butter and bake until crisp, turning several times; 3) spread with melted butter, sprinkle with grated Parmesan and bake until crisp.

BREAD FINGERS, ROUNDS, SQUARES, TRIANGLES, RINGS

Use whole wheat, white, rye, French bread, or paper-thin pumpernickel, slightly stale; spread with melted butter mixed with curry or poppy seeds or sesame seeds, or grated Parmesan and paprika. Bake in a very cool oven until crisp.

CORNUCOPIAS

Roll white bread, crusts removed, flat with rolling pin and spread with seasoned butter or any spread. Roll up from corner to corner, brush with melted butter and bake in a 250°F/Mark 1/2/130°C oven until golden, turning.

SPREADS: For 6 slices bread cut in rings, triangles or fingers, to be served with soup.

- Spread with 3 tablespoons butter, melted, beaten with 1 egg; roll in 1-1/2 cups freshly grated Parmesan cheese.

- Toast one side; spread untoasted side with herb butter: 4 ounces soft butter blended with 2 teaspoons each chives and parsley, 1/4 teaspoon each basil, marjoram or oregano, and tarragon. Grill slowly.

- Melt 2-1/2 ounces butter slowly with 2 crushed garlic cloves, 2 tablespoons Worcestershire sauce and 1/2 teaspoon salt. Spread on bread and bake in a very cool oven 1 hour or until crisp and dry.

- Mushroom duxelle (see glossary) spread on untoasted side of bread and grilled. Make 1 cup for 6 pieces of bread.

CREAM CHEESE PUFFS

3 ounces cream cheese, softened
1-1/2 teaspoons grated onion
1 egg yolk, beaten
1/4 teaspoon salt
1/8 teaspoon each white pepper and garlic powder
1/8 teaspoon grated lemon peel
2 drops Tabasco

paprika
40 1-1/2-inch rounds of white or rye bread

Mix cheese, onion, egg yolk and seasonings; taste for salt.
Toast bread rounds on one side, spread untoasted side with cheese mixture and sprinkle with paprika.
Grill 5 inches from heat until puffy.

CHEDDAR PUFFS

8 tablespoons shredded sharp Cheddar cheese
4 tablespoons very finely chopped mild onion
1 teaspoon very finely chopped green pepper
4 tablespoons mayonnaise
2 drops Tabasco
1/8 teaspoon garlic powder

paprika
30 1-1/2-inch rounds of white or rye bread

Mix cheese, onion, green pepper, mayonnaise, Tabasco and garlic powder; taste for salt.
Toast one side of bread rounds, spread untoasted side with cheese mixture and sprinkle with paprika.
Grill 5 inches from heat until golden and puffy.

CHEESE SQUARES

1 tablespoon flour
1 egg, beaten
4 tablespoons milk
5 tablespoons grated mozzarella cheese
1/4 teaspoon salt
1/8 teaspoon black pepper
1/8 teaspoon grated lemon rind

3 - 4 slices bread, crusts removed
3 - 4 tablespoons butter

Gradually beat flour into egg; blend in milk, cheese, and seasonings.
Dip bread slices into batter and sauté in butter until golden, turning once.
Cut into quarters.

Glossary

If you have difficulty in finding oriental ingredients, the numbers after the items indicate that these foods should be obtainable from the suppliers given on page 185.

Age: Deep-fried puffy tofu (bean curd) sold in Japanese stores. 1, 2

Aji Oil: Japanese sesame oil, also called chili oil, highly seasoned with cayenne pepper. To make aji oil: heat 1/2 pint sesame (or peanut) oil until just hazy. Remove from heat and blend in 4 tablespoons cayenne. Cool and store in a screw-top jar.

Bean Curd: see Tofu

Bean-thread Noodles: Also called pea-starch and cellophane noodles; fine transparent Chinese noodles made from ground mung beans and sold in packets of looped skeins or sold fresh. 1, 2, 3

Bok Choy: Chinese cabbage available in summer only. 3

Canned Bamboo Shoot Tips. 2

Chinese Black Beans: available dried or canned. 2, 3

Chinese Chives: Flat-leaf chives with a slight garlic flavor. Easily grown.

Dried Seaweed: see Kombu

Filé Powder: Powdered sassafras leaves used to thicken Creole dishes such as gumbos. If it is not available, substitute cornflour as a thickener and add a pinch of thyme for flavor.

Fish Soy: Chinese bottled fish sauce with the consistency of sesame oil. 2, 3

Fresh Bamboo Shoots: also available in cans. 3

Fresh Chinese Turnip: occasionally available. 3

Fuzzy Melon: occasionally available. 3

Fungus, Black: Chinese tree fungus, also called cloud ear or wood ear. Irregularly shaped, it expands to 5 or 6 times the original size when soaked, and becomes gelatinous and slippery in texture.

Glutinous Chinese Rice. 1, 2, 3

Glutinous Chinese Rice Flour. 1, 2, 3

Gobo: Burdock root. A long, thin, brown root, available fresh, canned or dried in Japanese stores. 1, 2

Goey Gaw: Blown-up dried fish stomach, sold in Chinese stores. 3

Hoisin Sauce: Thick, dark, Chinese sauce made of soy beans, chili, spices and garlic. Soy sauce and ketchup may be used as a substitute.

Kamaboko: Japanese steamed loaf made of fish forcemeat. Available canned, deep-frozen or dried. 1, 2

Katsuobushi: Japanese dried bonito flakes. 1, 2

Kim Chee: Oriental pickled cabbage, sold in jars or cans. Sauerkraut may be substituted. 1, 2, 3

Kombu: Dried sheet kelp used for making dashi (Japanese stock). 1, 2

Lop Chiang: Chinese pork sausages. Available canned. 3

Lotus Root: Water-lily root, available canned or dried in oriental stores. Dried roots almost triple in size when soaked. 1, 2, 3

Matsutakefu: Japanese dried wheat flour cakes. 1, 2

Mirin: Japanese sweetish *sake* (rice wine) used only for cooking. 1, 2

Miso (Akamiso — red, Shiromiso — white): Japanese fermented bean paste, available in packets. 1, 2

Mushroom Duxelle: Mushroom paste. Simmer very finely chopped mushrooms and stems in butter with finely chopped shallots. When very thick, season to taste; sprinkle with flour and add cream to make a thick mixture.

Mushrooms, Chinese: Dried black (winter) mushrooms with a distinctive flavor. They must always be soaked before use.

Name-take: Tiny Japanese mushrooms with stems. Sold bottled. 1, 2

Needles, Golden: These are the dried buds and stems of the lily (tiger lily) sold in bundles in Chinese stores. They have a musky, sweetish scent.

Oyster Sauce: Thick, oyster-flavored sauce used in Chinese cooking.

Oysters, Dried: Small dried Chinese oysters with concentrated flavor.

Seaweed: Dried kelp, bulk or sheets, available in Oriental stores and some health food shops. It doubles in size when soaked.

Shichimi: Japanese 7-seasoning pepper. 1, 2

Shingiku: Japanese dried chrysanthemum leaves. Not to be confused with garden chrysanthemums, although they are similar in appearance. 2

Shirataki: Thin Japanese yam-thread noodles.

Shrimps, Dried: Tiny dried shrimps frequently used in Oriental cooking for their pungent, concentrated flavor. 2, 3

Somen: Japanese thin noodles. 1, 2, 3

Tangerine Peel, Dried: Dried tangerine, mandarin orange or orange peel with a concentrated flavor.

Tofu: Bean curd (not paste). A smooth, bland, creamy custard made of puréed soy beans pressed into cakes. Widely used in both Chinese and Japanese cooking.

Tofu, Dried: Bean curd pressed into thin, flat sheets and dried.

Turnip Greens, Dried: Chinese turnips and tops preserved with salt, dried and rolled. Not to be confused with dried turnips. 3

Udon: Thick wheat noodles. 1, 2, 3

Winter Melon: 3

Wonton Skins: Available fresh or in packets. 1, 2, 3

1 Mikadoya, 3 & 4 Queensthorpe Mews, Queensthorpe Road, London SE26 4PN
2 Nippon Food Centre, Cydilda House, 61 Wimbledon High Street, Wimbledon Common, London SW19 5EE
3 Oriental Stores, 5 Macclesfield Street, Soho, London W.1.

Weights & Measures

The recipes in this book were originally devised and tested using American cup and spoon measures. These have been converted to fractions of pounds, ounces and pints where it seemed most practical. However, in some cases, where comparative volumes are more important to the success of a dish, the original cup measures have been retained.

The American cup holds 8 fluid ounces, the equivalent of a medium-sized teacup, and 2 cups, or 16 fluid ounces, make 1 American pint. (The Imperial pint holds 20 fluid ounces, or one-fifth more, and whenever pints have been used it is the 20-ounce pint that is meant.) However, provided the same cup is used throughout a recipe, a slight discrepancy will not matter. What is important is that cups, tablespoons and teaspoons should always be measured level.

For those who wish to use metric measures, the equivalents, adjusted to the nearest convenient figure, are as follows (volume and weight).

Should you wish to make a more accurate conversion (particularly useful for baking, etc.), the exact equivalents are:

1 ounce	=	28.35 grammes
16 ounces	=	453.6 grammes
1 pint	=	568 millilitres
1 kilo	=	2.2 pounds
1 litre	=	1.76 pints
1 decilitre	=	100 millilitres

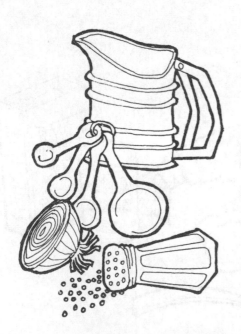

OUNCES/FLUID OUNCES		GRAMMES/MILLILITRES
½	=	15
1	=	25
2	=	50
3	=	75
4 (¼ pound)	=	100–110
5 (¼ pint)	=	150 (1½ decilitres)
6	=	175
7	=	200 (2 decilitres)
8 (½ pound)	=	225 (use ¼ kilo)
9	=	250 (2½ decilitres = ¼ kilo)
10 (½ pint)	=	275 (use 2½ decilitres)
11	=	300 (3 decilitres)
12	=	350 (3½ decilitres)
13	=	375
14	=	400 (4 decilitres)
15 (¾ pint)	=	425 (4½ decilitres)
16 (1 pound)	=	450 (4½ decilitres)
17	=	475
18	=	500 (5 decilitres = ½ kilo)
19	=	550 (5½ decilitres)
20 (1 pint)	=	575 (use 5½ decilitres)

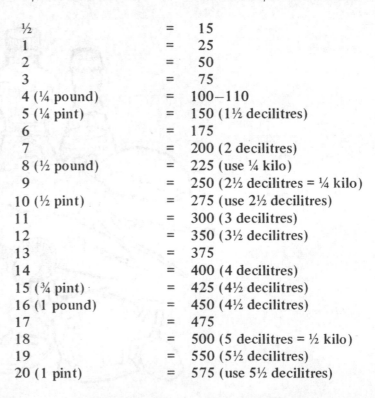

Index

About the Author

If one were to ask Coralie Davies Castle why cooking is so important to her, she would probably reply, "I guess it's just that I like to eat." But there are more complex reasons, too.

She claims to be a *hausfrau* from way back and recommends imaginative homemaking as an antidote to boredom and disillusionment with the outside world. She recalls spending hours as a small girl observing kitchen operations in her family's Kenilworth, Illinois, home, where she learned the tradition of German cookery.

However, it wasn't until she moved to Marin County, California, and started to explore San Francisco restaurants two and three times a week that food assumed its present importance in her life. After a year and nearly 200 restaurants, Mrs. Castle began trying to duplicate the recipes at home. She did not always succeed, but in the process of trying, she did develop delightful new dishes of her own. Encouraged by guests, family and friends she has seriously pursued cooking ever since, learning, originating, adapting, modifying and improving. Friends who have come to San Fran-

cisco from Indonesia, Brazil, Spain, Japan, Pakistan, Germany and other parts of the world added unusual ideas. Even her son contributed dishes from summers in Hawaii and Japan.

Second only to her kitchen is Coralie Castle's garden with its avocados, artichokes, seven kinds of citrus and a year-round supply of herbs and garnishes, as well as the usual fruits and vegetables.

Ten years ago, Mrs. Castle assisted in establishing the Marin Community Workshop for Retarded and Handicapped Adults. It was her desire to help the workshop, along with her personal crusade to spur individual creativity, that led to this book. A share of her author's royalties have gone to help meet the Workshop's urgent needs.

A superbly creative cook by instinct, Coralie Castle was trained by a German cook in her parents' home in Illinois. After moving to the San Francisco Bay area her knowledge of the foods of the world was expanded by the international potpourri of ethnic restaurants in that city and by yearly trips to Europe. Mrs. Castle is the co-author of four other cookbooks.